THE

HIGH

PRIESTESS

A WOLF IN THE LION'S DEN

BY

LINDSEY A. BRYANT,
LDS CONVERT

The High Priestess
A Wolf in the Lion's Den
Copyright © 2022 by Lindsey Ann Bryant

To request permissions, contact the publisher at
freedomhousepublishingco@gmail.com or contact@lindseybryantbranding.com
Hardcover ISBN: 978-1-952566-52-3
Paperback ISBN 978-1-952566-56-1
Audible ISBN: 978-1-952566-53-0
Printed in the USA.
Freedom House Publishing Co
Middleton, ID 83644
www.freedomhousepublishingco.com

FREEDOM HOUSE
PUBLISHING CO

DEDICATION

I dedicate this book to all the women who were murdered for using their voices to speak words that were ahead of their time. May my voice travel through space and time to find you.

I dedicate this book to my Heavenly Mother, my earthly mother, sisters, ancestors, daughters, progeny, and the women who will find this book long after I leave the earth.

Special consideration for the women in the Mastermind I was in while writing this book. To Keira Poulsen, my coach and mentor—I could not have accomplished this feat as quickly without your gifts.

I dedicate this book to my father-in-law, Donald Bryant, who told me that I had to write a book before his passing. I have felt your presence holding space for me and appreciate your help in this process.

I dedicate this book to J. Gary Duncan, my brilliant and resilient grandfather who loved the Church his whole life.

I dedicate this book to my past, present, and highest self.

I dedicate this book to the Church of Jesus Christ of Latter-day Saints.

I know this Church is true.

Lastly, I dedicate this book to the OG worldwide visionary, Joseph Smith.

The High Priestess

TABLE OF
CONTENTS

FOREWORD

What a brilliant time it is to be a woman. Being free to speak, write, and share what God is asking us to bring into the world is a holy privilege that I will never take for granted.

This was not always the case for women.

This was not the case for women like Marguerite Porete, who wrote a sacred book in the early 14th century. This book, called *The Mirror of Simple Souls*, broke the illusion of who God was and instead brought a new truth. This truth is that God is love and that love is God.

She was called a heretic for circulating a "book of lies," and was forced to watch her book burn at her feet. Later, she was burned at the stake for heresy.

Then, of course, there was Joan of Arc. The warrior who didn't ask to be a warrior, but when God called her, she put both feet firmly on the ground and never looked back. She led an army and she was directed by God in every action that she took. She spoke the bold and fearless words, "I am not afraid. I was born to do this."

Even after all that she did for France, Joan was eventually burned at the stake for heresy and dressing like a man.

I honor these women for their wisdom, their brilliance, and their courage. And these women are not alone.

There are many who have walked these paths. Very few names are known of the courageous women who came before us. We don't know their names because their names were burned with them. The stories of these fierce women were lost in the ashes.

But these women were sacred women. Women who were willing to risk everything for what they knew to be true.

We have the fables, stories, and mythology of the goddesses—like the great Isis, Kaun Yin, Tara, Kali, and more. These seem to be myths because their stories weren't written in the holy texts that humanity holds as proof of a person's existence in history. But these women were as real as you and I are. They led with power and faith and fully embodied their wisdom and gifts.

These women are here to help us rise in our gifts and our roles as mothers, teachers, healers, and leaders.

Because NOW is the time we change the script.

It is the first time that women can speak boldly, write fearlessly, and know that these books will never be burned again.

This is a sacred time to be a woman.

It is my belief that God has always and will always talk to humans. The only time God is quiet is when we choose to place the wall of fear, disbelief, or anger between us and God. We are the ones who hold the key to direct communion with the Divine. And when we choose to open that channel of receiving, miracles pour down from the heavens.

It is my belief that Lindsey chose to open that door up to receive this book. I am honored to have been Lindsey's sacred writing coach as she wrote this book. I witnessed her as she broke down the walls between her and God and willingly received this book.

I believe Lindsey is a steward of this message. She is the vessel from which it came through to bring light to those who read it. I honor her courage and faith.

Lindsey opens the gates for more women to rise and listen to the messages that are being sent to earth.

I believe this book will make ripples in time, reminding women of who they truly are. Messengers, angels, healers, leaders, and partners with God.

This is the most brilliant time to be a woman. I celebrate that this marvelous book is being published here and now. I celebrate you, Lindsey, and the work you are here to do.

Keira Poulsen

Founder of Freedom House Publishing Co.
Sacred Writing Coach

The High Priestess

A HIGH PRIESTESS

To be a High Priestess means to be a woman acting within the bounds of her own sovereignty.

A High Priestess is connected to Source and unapologetically expresses the messages given to her through her oneness with God. Her marriage with the Divine comes before anything else in her life.

A High Priestess recognizes her sacred calling and is dedicated to providing depth of knowledge for those who cross her path. Her devotion is towards the service of enlightenment so that others can understand their true purpose on earth.

A High Priestess dedicates her existence to cycles of renewal in her own body by way of healing. She seeks to separate herself from the ideologies that oppress all humans. Where there is injustice, she speaks out to create change.

A High Priestess utilizes the resonance of her voice for all things. She understands that a connection with Heavenly Mother, the earth, and various methods of somatic experiences are necessary to further the soul's progression in this life.

A High Priestess is a master of self and the inner environment. She turns inward for what she needs and finds unity with God within herself.

The High Priestess

PERMISSION TO WRITE THIS BOOK

I have tried to ignore this book. I have asked that God give this work to someone else. I have avoided and procrastinated this calling. But, like all things meant for me, this book has continued tapping on my shoulder. This book has demanded that I write it.

God has made it known to me that this book is one of the purposes of my existence. Upon receiving this knowledge, I recognize that my previous avoidance of writing originates from wanting to limit the power of God simply because I am defined as a human being.

I realize that my trepidation comes from fear conditioning in my DNA. Much like the epigenetics behind phobias, the genetic memory of witch trials and physical suffering for speaking a woman's truth all combines to try to stop my voice.

I feel the energy of God's jealousy toward me that I'd have the arrogance to place my limited knowledge above His limitlessness. I feel empathy for human beings who have been doing the same thing since the beginning of time—thinking they know better than God.

I think about Moses. I think about him walking into the top ancient city of Egypt built on the foundation of human blood and millennia. I think about Moses walking toward the intimidating height of this imperial city to free an entire race of enslaved people with a speech impediment, his brother, and a wooden staff.

How impossible would that have been to accomplish without the power of God assisting him? The Bible is full of proof of God's power harnessed by human beings to deliver miracles through impossible feats.

This same access to God's power is not a distant memory or a fairytale only available to characters in the Bible. Access to God's power is open to me right now, in this time, to accomplish my own life's purpose. I refuse to accept that I am not a powerful being simply because I was born a female. I dissent against the construct that women cannot hold court equal with men. I give myself permission to embrace my nature toward the transmutation of energy toward positive change.

An image of a temple flashes into my mind's eye. I am reminded that I am endowed with the blessings of covenants that I made in a temple. I am gifted with priesthood power and have access to God's power. I will be exercising my priesthood power in the act of co-creation with my Heavenly Parents (both divine masculine and divine feminine energies) to bring this book through my hands.

As I am a tremendous creative expression of two divine Heavenly Parents, I will create with the union of masculine and feminine energies within my body. I will constantly be clearing my body of lack or scarcity mindsets and old patterns of thinking to receive Source energy in alignment as a sacred vessel of light to educate. I am choosing to continually walk forward in faith. I am a walking miracle. I intend to let this book be a miracle—a great expression of my love for the Church of Jesus Christ of Latter-day Saints.

I am here, willing to be led in the direction I must go. I am choosing obedience to the will of my Father in Heaven. I am giving myself permission to lean into this calling.

I feel a wave of assurance. I am more evident to myself.

I am qualified. I am qualified to do this work because I have been created for it.

I am qualified to speak on these sacred topics because I have worked to align myself with the highest order of truth. I am qualified to labor this information into this book because I have practiced the concepts to the point of cellular healing of my past traumas.

I am qualified to birth this book into the 3D realm because this book is already alive within my consciousness. I have been nurturing its growth. I am a light vessel—strong enough to survive the result of fecundation.

I am qualified to speak because I have a voice.

I am qualified to speak about Heavenly Mother and what it means for women to hold priesthood power because I am an endowed female member utilizing priesthood power daily. I am qualified to teach light warfare because I have survived many spiritual and mental wars in my lifetime. I am free enough from shame to say that I have been guilty in the past of mastering the adversary's weaponry to accomplish my own selfish desires. Now that I am a light warrior, I can teach others how to fight against these weapons of destruction.

I am qualified because I am an evolved warrior in a constant state of shedding earthly limitations in the act of remembrance of who I was before I came to my mortal probation. I am a different sort of creature. I am qualified to write this book to provide the armor of God to the minds of my brothers and sisters because I know this territory well. I am a calibrated weapon in the hands of my Father.

I AM.

I am a high priestess.

I am a sovereign of the warrior tribe of Benjamin.

I am a weapon against the adversary.

I am a container of Source energy.

I am a powerful woman.

I am qualified.

God has called me.

I am choosing to accept my calling.

God's grace will be sufficient to cover the rest.

As it always has been and always will be–

Because God is ALWAYS who He says He is.

God IS the great

"I AM."

There is no higher seat of authority than that of my living God.

WHAT THIS
BOOK IS NOT

As important as it is to discuss what this book is, it is equally important to assert what this book is not.

This book is not me asking for your permission.

This book is NOT an invitation for men or brethren to come out of the woodwork and dim down to me what it means for me, as a woman, to exercise or hold priesthood power.

If you are a man reading this, I invite you to practice your listening skills as you seek to understand an experience different from the one you currently have. Your sisters, wives, mothers, ancestors, and progeny need your efforts to help us enact positive change.

Anytime I have brought up this topic with male members of The Church of Jesus Christ of Latter-day Saints (save but a few select men), I have been cut off from speaking with "WELL…" as the opening line. I wouldn't begin to know about your experience as your gender in this world outside of what I have witnessed with my eyes or heard from males as they relay their personal life experiences.

This book is NOT me adding fuel to the fire with those who seek to take the Church down. I love this Church and that's why I am dismantling certain aspects of it to examine how we can make it function more appropriately. I am acting as an advocate for female members of this Church by exercising my voice. (From this point forward, anytime I mention "the Church" or "church," I am referencing The Church of Jesus Christ of Latter-day Saints)

This book is NOT me stating I have ALL of the answers to all questions. Receiving all revelation about these sacred topics is not confined to my book deadline. I fully anticipate that I will continue to receive answers long after this book has been published. I encourage anyone reading this to petition God on your own behalf to know the truth for yourself.

I am confident I will still have questions that will pop up throughout the rest of my life. The answers to those questions will demand me to develop and align to be able to know them.

So far, what answers I have received have been divinely given as rewards for my faithfulness.

This book is me answering some of the questions that Church leaders should ask female members of the Church.

It's like I tell my personal branding clients who are structuring businesses around their client needs: "Smarter, not harder. If you want to know what your ideal client needs from you as a product or service provider, ASK them."

This Church is an ultimate service provider in this life and the next. It is imperative to continue to make improvements for more satisfactory experiences.

ABOUT ME

I am a mid-thirties female convert to The Church of Jesus Christ of Latter-day Saints. My life was a myriad of insurmountable, traumatic experiences until I decided to become a member of the Church. I am free of shame when I say that my choices while in survival mode were not upstanding. I forgive myself for the ways that I was forced to survive. I continue to forgive myself as I ascend to new heights of wisdom and, subsequently, fresh grief of my past choices. I am not perfect and I have made my mistakes. When I know better, I adjust and do better.

I have overcome an alcohol dependency and have been sober for three years now. As I held past versions of myself in this life in my mind's eye free of judgment and paralleled them with biblical analysis of the Apostle Paul, it has been made clear to me that my past is now serving a much larger purpose. I hold a knowing that my past is a deepening shadow for understanding the darkness of others so that I can aid in spiritual breakthroughs. My past has also propelled the forward movement of my present and future selves. It will help me on my path to becoming a great metaphysician, like the Apostle Paul was.

WHAT IS A METAPHYSICIAN?

It all begins within the thoughts of our minds. Jesus and the Apostle Paul were humans who were able to access and harness the transformative power of God. They then utilized their word choice to ask for miracles. The power of their words, unified with the power of God, was then channeled through their hands to perform miracles of physical healing on other people. The use of physics, understanding the importance of divine masculine and divine feminine energies, and accessing the power of God to perform these miracles was an example of what is possible for each of us in this life. I believe that each of us can become like our Savior, not just in demeanor and with our actions, but also in performing miracles to heal ourselves and others.

Through the first three decades of my life, I searched for truth in many different forms of belief systems, non-beliefs, paganism, scientific evidence, nihilism, atheism, shamanism, and earthbound religions. My life experiences, mainly composed of moments living outside of alignment, have led me to the eternal truths I will write about. I will not defile the beliefs of others with this book. I want to show the interconnectedness ALL belief systems share, which are simply Universal Truths as we can grasp them. I will be highlighting these similarities to illuminate the mind's eye to the very unique LDS concept of priesthood power.

I must also share that I have had health issues for several years. The source of these health issues finally came to light while writing this book. The initial diagnosis of my health problems was fibromyalgia; however, the core issue turned out to be a benign pituitary brain tumor. I am still astounded that the trauma that I have been through in my life resulted in a literal tumor in my mind.

Before this diagnosis, I had a vision of a black mass in my physical body during a meditation. I do not believe it was a coincidence that this was discovered when it was. I was already researching various holistic healing methods at that time. I started practicing self-healing in spiritual practice alongside prescription medication to reduce the size of the tumor. I also began utilizing these methods to help my personal branding clients heal to step into their power as entrepreneurs. My spiritual practices enhance my business capabilities. A woman stepping into financial abundance is a sacred rite of passage. I am happy to integrate all aspects and versions of myself to be the best for everyone I encounter.

The transformative ability to heal me and others comes from the teachings of Jesus Christ, who was the greatest metaphysician who ever walked the earth. The Church has provided me with a spiritual outline to follow as I dig deeper and fill in the concepts that help me draw closer to following Jesus in His same path. The Church teachings have been further validated as I hungrily absorbed information from various scholars, academics, historians, religious beliefs, and more. The Church of Jesus Christ of Latter-day Saints has become a spiritual Ivy League school that has quenched a thirst for knowledge in me.

I have never been satisfied with surface textbook answers to my questions. There is still too much ambivalence and blind following around priesthood power, especially concerning women and the priesthood, its true meaning, and the potential we possess when exercising priesthood power. As taboo as my methods may be, I will be going back into ancient history to analyze examples of ancient "priestesses" and their roles within societies and culture to add meaning to Latter-day Saint female members holding priesthood power.

We will have some "come to Jesus" conversations in this book. I am someone who usually finds 100 ways not to do something before I catch on to the correct way. I am also someone who has found out what something truly means by understanding what it is not. I must address how I have seen that aspects of operations are *not* working in the current church culture to show the contrast of how things can be.

I was brought into this Church by God to be a changemaker, wave bringer, energy shifter, and great healer. Change doesn't happen unless people get honest and have difficult conversations to reach resolutions. We must address the shadow work in the Church and the world to heal it. Much like a doctor needs to know symptoms before a treatment plan can be developed and executed to create a better quality of life, we can't treat the disease of lack or limited thinking in The Church of Jesus Christ of Latter-day Saints if we don't know its symptoms.

It is crucial to stay open-minded while reading this book. I have found evidence that supports my unraveling of fear-based thinking that causes unnecessary division in our church culture.

I do not subscribe to the belief that truth is just this ONE thing I can hold in my hand. It is my belief that:

Truth is this *and* that *and* that. Truth is a multidimensional, multifaceted window of interconnectedness to *all things*. I doubt the human mind can even fully comprehend the magnitude of the truth we need to accept to change things toward Joseph Smith's highest ideal when he sought to establish this Church on earth.

Components of truth can be discovered in various facets of life, through many methods, and even in the observance of opposing life experiences to the ones we choose for ourselves.

It is not enough to just know something to be true. At a certain point in maturity, it is the responsibility of individuals to claim rites of passage. "Claiming power" or "claiming rites of passage" are terms equal to the action commonly termed "striving" in church language. Faith and pursuit are required on our part. Faith is not a waiting word; it is an action word. It requires our willingness to take step after step in a forward motion. Faith is surrendering the raw power of our subconscious mind to be molded by the interconnected all-knowing of the super-conscious mind/higher self/God.

I believe that when we, as human beings, walk forward in faith, we create momentum with our intent. When we choose to step forward, the law of grace, made possible by the Atonement of Jesus

Christ, clicks into place and Heavenly Mother connects us with all of the mysteries of the universe. She allows us to receive revelation or answers to what we strive to understand from Heavenly Father.

She is the physics that literally brings heaven to connect with earth. She is also in the way we "ground" our body into the present moment to hear personal revelation.

I am a convert to the Church who has reached the crowning ordinance of temple sealing. In a separate ordinance that took place the month before my sealing, I was able to take out my endowments. In later chapters, I will explain more about those ordinances and how they pertain to priesthood power. I began noticing connections and similarities of past life studies as I have progressed through the refining disciplines of Church teachings to be worthy to receive these temple ordinances. I have found universal truths in many types of belief systems. For me, The Church of Jesus Christ of Latter-day Saints has been the most complete library of Universal Truth I have been able to find. It will take me my whole life to read the entire spiritual library of the Church.

I want other women to know our Heavenly Mother, and I believe many women are lost because not much exists in the English language about Heavenly Mother. From my study for this book, I have concluded that a mix of Western ideology, worldly forms of patriarchal structure related to the Hammurabi codes, and poor translation of Hebrew scriptures into the bastardized English language are responsible for Heavenly Mother being erased.

While none of the information I will bring forth within these pages will be original, I believe that the way I make connections between these sources of information will offer a better comprehensive understanding of priesthood power. This is not a book of ladder definitions, and I am curious if linear thinkers will be attuned to the way I speak. I speak the language of the soul when I am in my super-conscious mind, and not all of this book will be straight facts and logic. I have been instructed by divine guidance to use logic and intuition with this book.

I will be providing insight into the personal revelation that I have received. I receive divine guidance in many different ways.

I would like to share the experience of how I decided to write this book.

The seed of curiosity was planted in my mind when I heard the current prophet (the President of the Church), Russell M. Nelson, express to women that it was vital for us to understand what it means for women to have priesthood power. I began asking, "What does it mean for women to have priesthood power?" I received a lot of puzzled looks and vague answers.

I asked missionaries the same question when the time came for me to take temple preparation classes before my endowment session. They sweetly and humbly gave me similar answers to what I had received before and said, "I do not know more than that on the topic."

I stepped forward in faith to take out my endowments and trusted that God would provide answers as I kept asking questions. One day, I was deep in prayer and I petitioned Heavenly Father to answer my questions about what it meant for a woman to have priesthood power. I immediately received an answer to this prayer. He revealed to me that I would write a book on Heavenly Mother and what it means for women to have priesthood power.

I was highly puzzled by this answer. How was I going to write a book about something I knew very little about? It has been said that the best way to become a master is to start by being a student. Writing this book has been a fast course through the spiritual Ivy League that has elevated me to facilitate my own healing at cellular levels. In a short timeframe, researching and writing this book have strengthened my testimony of the necessity of faith to walk forward into the wilderness to do the work that God has called me to do. I have a renewed respect for Joseph Smith. I have new eyes seeing what my Savior went through on an intimate level.

This book is one of the purposes of my life. As an expansively creative visionary, I am attempting to utilize my logic, intuition, and personal revelation toward a divine marriage of masculine and feminine energies to assist others in following Christ in the teachings that enabled Him to perform physical miracles during his ministry. I believe that this work, anchored in my purpose, will change a dynamic and old narrative between the male and female members of The Church of Jesus Christ of Latter-day Saints for the better.

Receiving my patriarchal blessing in my second year after my conversion became a tool that I have used to pry into my core understanding of who I am and my life's purpose here on earth. These blessings are sacred and to be protected. I prayed every morning before I sat down to write this book and asked God to reveal what I needed to register. One of the revelations from my patriarchal blessing is that I am assigned to the tribe of Benjamin. While the tribe is the smallest of the 12 tribes of Israel, Benjamites have massive manifesting capabilities. I will talk more about the promise of the tribe of Benjamin and its significance later in this book.

Similar to the Apostle Paul (another great convert from the tribe of Benjamin), my past and pain will serve to illustrate a greater depth of the transformative powers of discipleship and LDS priesthood power. I take confidence that I share a sigil with the Apostle Paul, who was an exceptional writer, a metaphysician, and a force for change. Practicing self-mastery has led me closer to his ministry and to Jesus Christ.

There exists a need to understand female priesthood power at a metaphysical level. At a subatomic particle level. At a shaping reality "out there" level. And at an epigenetic level to eradicate generational sin in our literal DNA for future generations.

There will be shifts and energetic output in our body once we awaken and exercise this priesthood power; scientific measurement of activating supernatural power as evidenced in *Becoming Supernatural* by Dr. Joe Dispenza.

Ultimately, women have the power to choose their birthrights in the Church. Birthright, from a Biblical stance, is passed from the father to the firstborn son. The father could choose to go against this and give it to a younger son. If the father refused his birthright, his son took double for birthright inheritance. Both his father's and his.

As evidenced in scripture, the work does not change. If one man or woman refuses their work on this earth to carry out their specific purpose, the work gets passed on to someone able and willing to fulfill these purposes. The natural upheaval of truth is a cycle that continues to revolve only to be pushed back down and silenced. We're running out of time to keep repeating similar cycles if this Church will fulfill its mission as the restored gospel of our Lord and Savior, Jesus Christ.

I stood outside of the Idaho Falls temple in March of 2019 and was met by a female ancestor who told me that I was to receive a birthright by becoming a member of The Church of Jesus Christ of Latter-day Saints. My mother left the Church as an adolescent. I had no knowledge of what that birthright meant at the time and am sure I have only begun to come into the light of understanding the full details of it. As I now sit with the diligent pursuit of striving to reach my full stature, I know that I have taken on the purpose of not only myself but that of my mother, who unlinked the chain of our ancestral rights in evolving the Church.

I am a modern pioneer in the quest that my ancestors in early church history began when they left everything they knew in European countries because a united vision of restoring the gospel burned in their hearts. They started the work. I am here to carry my birthright passed on to me from them. Many LDS communities' cultural acceptances and practices standard have pushed members out of the Church, created false realities around what the Church is anchored in, and tarnished what priesthood power means to females. We have limitless potential for co-creation with God when a woman who understands her priesthood power pairs with an enlightened man who properly utilizes his priesthood power. Too much of the world in Church communities is slipping us into comfortable, box-checking ambivalence of our purpose and power as seeds of our Heavenly Parents.

Your distraction from the world and leaving the work to the next generation is fine with the devil. It does his job for him.

I'm here to tell you the culture of the Church that leaves so many drowning in plain sight is the infiltration of evil and we are allowing it.

Fear is not a virtue. Neither is garment policing. It is not yet complete if your charity and compassion do not extend to yourself.

Women policing women, so men don't have to erode the purpose of Relief Society. There is a difference between shame and guilt. There is a difference between accountability and judgment.

It is not enough for us to allow certain aspects of this culture to continue.

The Church of Jesus Christ of Latter-day Saints is unique from all other Christian religions. If you have not heard of the Church before, I am excited to share more. If you are a current member or someone who already knows the Church, I hope this expands your understanding of this religion. I hope that this book will help you actualize your purpose and potential regardless of who you are or where you're at with your spiritual progression.

The High Priestess

INTRODUCTION

The Great War in Heaven that took place in our premortal existence was not a war of swords and flesh. It was a war on the mind. It was a war of distorted thinking, fear, and disobedience to God's will. Similarly, in mortal existence, the mind is the target of the adversary to shut us out from actualizing our potential during our time in physical bodies on this earth.

The adversary wishes to gain our consent to misuse our inherent soul gifts toward manifesting his agenda rather than God's. The mind can be closed from receiving power in many ways, such as fear, dysregulation of the nervous system, shame, social rejection, and limitations brought on by scarcity mindsets, to name just a few.

It is an act of spiritual warfare for the mind to be attacked, closed, or unclear. The Bible provides a transparent definition of our armor for withstanding the weaponry of the adversary in Ephesians 6:11-18 KJV. This is how it is defined (the statements in parentheses are my thoughts):

"Put on the whole armour of God, that ye may be able to stand against the wiles of the devil. For we wrestle not against flesh and blood, but against principalities, against powers, against the rulers of the darkness of this world, against spiritual wickedness in high places. Wherefore take unto you the whole armour of God, that ye may be able to withstand in the evil day, and having done all, to stand. Stand therefore, having your loins girt about with truth (chastity covenants), and having on the breastplate of righteousness ("high priest" breastplate covered in gemstones thought to protect

1

the vital organs of the body and help aid in receiving revelation from God); And your feet shod with the preparation of the gospel of peace (not giving in to letting outside influences change your internal climate.); Above all, taking the shield of faith (a mind rooted in abundant surrender not scarcity), wherewith ye shall be able to quench all the fiery darts of the wicked. And take the helmet of salvation (protection of the third-eye and crown chakras), and the sword of the Spirit, which is the word of God (revelation, both personal and collectively): Praying always with all prayer and supplication in the Spirit, and watching thereunto with all perseverance and supplication for all saints."

The full armor of God, as highlighted in Ephesians, consists of several methods of protection for the mind and spirit. Both the mind and spirit are gatekeepers of physical health.

In our mortal lives, the mind is how God's power can be received by the body when it is open. The receptiveness of our mind then influences all of the other energy centers of the body, our physical health, and the miracles we can give to the world we live in. The Church of Jesus Christ of Latter-day Saints is so great with the "Om," "Divine Masculine," or "I know" in the form of spiritual ascension principles and practices.

I see members burn out a lot because of not understanding the divine feminine "Lam" or "I am" or grounding aspects necessary to recover from burnout by being present in the now. Grounding is in the initial ordinance acts, for example, immersion by water, laying on of hands in the blessing methods, and ordinances practices in the temple. Daily grounding practices need to be taught to regulate the various nervous systems in the body. The balancing of the masculine energy of intellectual pursuit is the equal practice of somatic experiences of the body to recover from going into heavenly realms of ascension again.

I believe that it is no coincidence that the crowning ordinance in The Church of Jesus Christ of Latter-day Saints (the ordinance of the temple sealing of the family) sits in the highest part of the temple structure, closest to God. The physical space where temple sealings occur in the temple mimics the body's crown chakra or energy center.

The crown chakra connects to higher consciousness or state of being in many other religions and belief systems. In the LDS religion, the sealing of spouses and the family enacts an initiation of heightened priesthood power with the union of masculine and feminine priesthood holders. Eternal marriage of the spouses through temple sealing is an ordinance that mirrors the divine marriage of God and Heavenly Mother. The unity of divine feminine and divine masculine energies is a story that echoes throughout world history.

Priesthood power is literal access to the power of God. Priesthood power, as it relates to the concepts and principles of The Church of Jesus Christ of Latter-day Saints, is a power that requires mastery of a mind free from lack and limitations.

The Church of Jesus Christ of Latter-day Saints needs vocal converts who will offer their perspective to implement and update resources that support the new members better. With divorce rates in the Church now mirroring secular divorce rate statistics, many members of blended families are not receiving the crucial support needed to make their families successful. Currently, resources and education in bishopric handbooks do not exist toward supporting the blended family dynamic.

I have seen many areas of conflict and segregation within church culture as a convert to the Church who is also a female priesthood holder governing a blended family. I have experienced added stressors to my marriage and life due to unique aspects of being a new member and new spouse within a church culture

3

dynamic that is, frankly, unrighteous dominion. I am not an attorney but have experienced meddling from my "ward family" that I can plainly see violates legal custody agreements signed by a civil judge.

There is currently a mass exodus of members alongside members becoming inactive because of hypocrisy or abuse of some kind experienced through church culture that the members have adopted over time. "The Family: A Proclamation to the World," which resides at the core of the religious mission, has become a toxic cultural war against the blended family, with worldly patriarchy and Western ideology as the primary fuel for the fire. I have been tempted to leave the Church already, and my issues have damaged my marriage.

Many will not speak up. I am not that kind. Before I go into depth about the topics in this book, I need to add on to what this book is NOT. This book is not about my disdain for The Church of Jesus Christ of Latter-day Saints. It is not anger at God for what fallible people have done. This is my petition to truly understand this religion for what it is and our potential within the confines of safe spaces held by the Church. If we are brothers and sisters in Christ and cannot spar or grapple with challenging topics on occasion, we need better respect for one another. I believe that silence in place of speaking about hard things is the same as a lie. The attitude of passivity is a tool of the adversary.

I titled this book *The High Priestess* because that title is what I have ascended to in my spiritual stature because of the Church. Through my spiritual journey, I have healed a broken relationship attachment style. I have overcome addictions to alcohol, abuse, and trauma. I have aided my body and mind to recover from the trauma resulting in a diagnosis of fibromyalgia and a pituitary brain tumor. I have experienced a transformative power that exists when a woman actualizes and understands what it means to have priesthood power. Now I am stepping into healing others and helping guide them in the spiritual journey of this life.

Christ and the Apostle Paul led by example, showing us how we can utilize our words and access God's power to heal the physical body. There is a science to change and conversion. The physics of priesthood power will be talked about in this book.

The female version of a priest is a priestess. The Shekhinah in Jewish theology is the glory of the divine presence, conventionally represented as light or interpreted symbolically (in Kabbalism as a divine feminine aspect). Much about our Heavenly Mother and our potential as women is hidden in ancient history, female spiritual writings, and the Hebrew language.

I was born with spiritual gifts. They have been expanded on and magnified as I have progressed down the covenant path. I possess the inherent skills of visions and the ability to see spirits, angels, and dark entities. My favorite places on earth are the temples where I can stand as a proxy for the deceased for their sacred ordinances. The temples are also where members receive sacred ordinances for themselves. I genuinely believe Heavenly Mother's principal dwelling place is in temples, and I have visions of Her sitting on a throne in temples.

We are taught that God has a divine feminine equal partner, or Heavenly Mother, in the LDS religion. Not much is known about Heavenly Mother or female priesthood power in the LDS religion, even though we are told about these concepts. We also don't know much about the why of what we are told to do by Church leaders. Ambivalence and lack of education leave us wasting time and tripping through life as members.

What I really talk about with this book is the restorative power that the Atonement has to what was broken. A blended family is a form of restoration. The healing of cultural toxicity and generational trauma is a form of repair. Giving women avenues to stand and speak about their experiences is a form of restoration.

This is the restored church of Christ; we must acknowledge the places in the Church that are still breeding shame. Using the salve of the Atonement and the universal laws of grace, we can take the pain and refine it to remove imperfections and end with elements and weapons fashioned as the whole armor of God to protect our families.

In this way, Jesus has taken on another form of workmanship as a spiritual blacksmith. We always have the choice to alchemize the energies of pain through Christ's Atonement toward full body, mind, and spiritual healing in the refiner's fire.

ORDINANCES

Mystical marriage (the union of souls bound for all time and eternity) in The Church of Jesus Christ of Latter-day Saints is deemed "the crowning ordinance" in the temple. The crowning ordinance is the temple sealing of families to one another for time and all eternity. The sealing of a family together begins with sealing the man and woman in a holy marriage.

Before this sealing can be accomplished, members proceed through a temple ordinance called an endowment. The endowment is the ordinance that separates and prepares an individual for greater priesthood power. When an individual goes through their own endowment session, covenants are made with God that give them deeper access to God's power and our own priesthood power. I understand that a member of The Church of Jesus Christ of Latter-day Saints can obtain the temple ordinance of an endowment outside of marital proceedings. The endowment can be taken out in preparation for a mission or when an individual member feels it is necessary for their personal spiritual progression.

The covenants already made with God must be in good standing to enter into the new covenant of a temple sealing. A current temple recommendation, signed by a member's bishop and stake president must also be in place to enter the house of the Lord for an endowment ordinance. Energetically sacred spaces must be kept actively free of static that can be brought in by the inner chaos of unregulated bodies. Standards are important. Nervous system regulation is the main result of keeping covenants and adhering to the Word of Wisdom. The body is often called a vessel, but I would like to reframe that to: "The body is a vehicle."

If we think of the body in the way of being able to promote spiritual delivery to visit our Heavenly Parents, maybe we'd have a better attitude about the routine maintenance of the body through covenant keeping. The ordinances of The Church of Jesus Christ of Latter-day Saints are sacred, and so are the reasons why we keep our covenants.

Covenants (the two-way promises we make with God) and ordinances (the somatic experiences performed by male priesthood holders) are two-part verbal contracts.

Words make contracts with God. Words also have the ability to make agreements with dark entities to attach to people and spaces. You can then manifest answers, miracles, and revelation faster when your actions are aligned with your words.

I recommend that you to look up a talk by David A. Bednar from a Church Educational System fireside address delivered at Brigham Young University–Idaho on May 3, 2009. I have listened to this talk at least 50 times and keep making new discoveries about how the adversary and his fallen angels sneakily obtain our agreement to misuse our bodies and shut us off from entering the chariot of God. You can find this talk, entitled "Things as They Really Are," on YouTube or find the text version of the talk on churchofjesuschrist.org. I don't feel that merely quoting portions of the talk is sufficient for you to get the full power of his words. I encourage you to listen for yourself and ponder the meanings with the Holy Spirit flowing from his words.

I invite you to close your eyes and tune into your body. If you pray, ask that God reveal the truth from the scriptures that you need for your own progression and understanding.

I would like to include all of the scripture references from David A. Bednar's talk in this section. I am now inviting you to pick up the scriptures and study the following verses:

- Jacob 2:3 and 4:13
- D&C 121:45, 93: 24, 93:33-34, 88:15, 64:34-35, 88:118, 60:13, 76:94, 1:3, 82:3
- 1 Nephi 19:6, 17:45, 19:6
- Alma 7:12–13, 32:35, 41:3
- 1 Corinthians 3:16–17
- 2 Nephi 2:27
- Mosiah 2:36–37, 4:29-30
- 2 Nephi 28:21, 1:15
- Job 38:7
- 1 Thessalonians 4:4
- 2 Timothy 3:5
- Moses 5:30
- Proverbs 23:7
- Moroni 7:41
- Mormon 9:27-28
- Joseph Smith—Matthew 1:5, 33, 37

In his talk, Elder Bednar says that a high level of fidelity would enhance our experiences. The high fidelity to covenants brings a whisper of the Holy Spirit to the level of a SHOUT in our body awareness. Our regulated nervous systems should be high priority; which is to say that periods of time where we rest (like Sunday) should continue to be devoted to nervous system regulation and being open to receive.

The High Priestess

ENDOWMENTS

THE GIFT OF ACCESS

"So with woman: Her special gifts are
to be exercised for the benefit and uplift of the race."
-John A. Widstoe

M. Russell Ballard said, "When men and women go to the temple, they are both endowed with the same power, which by definition is priesthood power."

The temple ordinance called the "endowment" is how we receive the gift of deeper access to the power of God. The endowment ordinance is the method by which we obtain full access to priesthood power. Priesthood power is access to God's power to conduit into miracles, personal revelation, healing, etc.

We need not look farther than the scriptures to see and learn of examples of mortals utilizing God's power to manifest miracles.

Endowment ordinances in the temple are a modern-day transfiguration process for each individual. Transfiguration or "healing" is essential down to a cellular level to withstand the raw power of God, which runs through our organic bodies. It's like a plant in the correct type of sunlight exposure.

The transfiguration process is similar to the transfiguration Moses experienced on Mount Sinai when he looked upon God, Heavenly Mother, and Jesus in the burning bush, but in smaller doses. The endowment and principles of the covenant path are

11

essential for the high energetic output of such pure God energy through our physical bodies.

We must become tempered by the endowment ordinance and covenant-keeping to withstand heightened levels of transcendence on our path of spiritual progression.

I believe that "power," in the proper application of accessing God's power, taps into the root of the word "to be able." To be able is where autonomy comes into the game. The consistency with which we adhere to the covenants made during our temple endowments is equal to our human bodies' capacity to be filled with priesthood power. David A. Bednar said, "A high level of fidelity can enhance the experience."

Priesthood power from God gives us the ability to fulfill our divine right to bring miracles into physical manifestations abundantly.

I believe temple attendance is more about small feats of transfiguration than anything else. I also think about how we do work for the dead there. The temples have to act as vortex points for souls to show up in such numbers in those spaces. I have seen several disembodied souls show up to accept their ordinances when acting as a proxy for them.

There is to be a component of priesthood power that becomes initiated with death. I don't know what it means yet, but I will keep striving to understand. But one quote that came through to me while thinking about death and priesthood power was by Pres. Russell M. Nelson. He said, "Death is a necessary component of our spiritual progression."

Brigham Young also talked about passing into the spiritual realm; we possess a portion of God's power.

Here are two questions I will ask in prayer on this aspect of priesthood power, and I invite you to do the same:

How does death initiate us into further priesthood power?

What is the physics of death?

THE "P" WORD

History rings with cautionary stories of leaders gone manic and illustrations of the unrighteous dominion of few trampling the values and lives of many. If you ask someone about their free associations to the word "power," more times than not you will get a response similar to "control," "dominance," or some other method of unrighteous dominion. This is very important to consider as the practical application of power is preceded by how an individual defines the word in their mind.

Unrighteous dominion has been consistent with applying members in leadership or service roles in areas with toxic church culture under the guise of "priesthood power." Exertion of unrighteous dominion, control, or dominance over others with a church calling plants noxious seeds that eventually sprout and push the injured party out of the Church. But, in reality, it wasn't the Church or God who planted doubt, it was another fallible human being.

A false narrative under a culture of "permission" down a chain of authority is currently a rampant problem in modern-day "Zion." Exercising cheap power in the form of unrighteous dominion, *not* to be confused with priesthood power, has caused major divides between church doctrine and a toxic church culture that the members have adopted over time. Several aspects of this diseased thinking came to my attention through my own experience of coming into the Church in Boise, Idaho.

I realized even more issues through conversations I have had with women currently struggling with whether or not they should stay in the Church or women who have already left. Many members have warned me about speaking to people who have left. "Be careful," they say.

I want to challenge that and say that those are precisely the experiences that we should listen to, hold space for, and use as a springboard to implement change.

Now that I have shed light on what power is NOT, I would like to assemble the word's meaning. The root or etymology of the word "power" is the Latin "potere" which means "to be able."

"The powers that be" are those who hold authority (a common example in LDS context explained as "holding priesthood keys") and "authority behind the throne." That last part is so intriguing to me because of the geometric components which make up the shape of the energetic light centers of our bodies called chakras.

WHAT IS THE TRUE MEANING OF POWER?

"Behind the throne" is a term that refers to the people who exert influence on those with formal titles. They are the power behind the ones who seem to be in charge. As a verb, "power" is sometimes defined as "to supply with mechanical or electrical energy." What I have just outlined is crucial to keep in the forefront of the mind's eye as I dive farther into women holding priesthood power.

More definitions of power according to Vocabulary.com are:

1. (Noun) Possession of the qualities (especially mental qualities) required to do something or get something done.
2. (verb) Supply the force or power for the functioning of.

The real dirty "P" word isn't "power." It's the worldly form of "PATRIARCHY."

WHAT IS WORLDLY PATRIARCHY & WHERE DID IT COME FROM?

History, archeology, science, and psychology are all dripping with women's blood. Alongside the slaughter and violence toward women since the installation of the Code of Hammurabi in ancient Mesopotamia, raging sexism keeps women from being heard or studied correctly.

For example, archeologists have retold stories of Viking burial graves honoring women and tagged them as males. Female voices have been suffocated with the fear of physical violence for speaking truth, like in the cases of witch trials, Joan of Arc, and so many others.

Worldly patriarchy keeps the war between the male and female genders stoked. The emotional weapons of control used by each sex are different but equally damaging to the family structure. Sophisticated emotional weapons assigned to the sexes can be seen within the marital systems of members of the Church. The presence of control within marriage creates massive tension when attacking a spouse that our soul is tied to. We are energetically ripping ourselves apart. Therefore, the attack or manipulation of a relationship partner is also an act of self-harm.

I highly recommend watching a television series entitled "The Ascent of Woman" by historian Dr. Amanda Foreman to understand more about gender roles, rights, and the history of women's struggles within the patriarchy since the beginning of human existence.

WHAT DOES THAT LOOK LIKE AND MEAN NOW?

Gender stereotypes of men making money and women staying home to care for children have equipped the sexes with unfair control over each other, each assigned specific needs within the relationship dynamic. I am going to replace the word "power" with the word "control" as I explain this dynamic.

If a man's power or control is money, then the woman remains reliant on the male to care for her financially. As long as money is held as a control, the woman cannot progress, temporally or spiritually.

A woman's power, control, and worth in worldly patriarchal societies have always been sex or virginity. As long as sex is held as a control, the man cannot progress either.

Both sex and money are tools of deeper trust and connection that have been twisted into weapons of harm.

The war between the sexes then becomes male domination—controlling the woman with money—while the woman controls the man with the withholding or rationing out of holiday or baby-making-only sex. A woman may also use sex as a way to trap a man with a pregnancy he did not agree to. She may use sex as manipulation in other ways to get what she wants. A man may use money to threaten the woman to stay in a toxic relationship. He may use money to manipulate the woman in other ways. Women may take money from the man in an act of resentment. The man may commit nonconsensual sexual crimes toward the woman in his expression of resentment.

All of these examples are wrong and misuse the interdependence in a relationship that bonds a couple on new levels. These abusive dynamics cause marital disconnect that keeps couples from actualizing their potential together. The war of the sexes drives divorce and crime statistics higher.

Worldly patriarchy is a much more considerable accumulation of these toxic dynamics that penetrate the ecosystem of the earth. Worldly patriarchy is why the earth needs energetic healing from humans. In unbalanced states, the motivation men could use to build an earthly legacy instead creates a war of control against women's bodies. The state of emotional security of a woman is powerful in creation as the first spark of life occurs when an egg and sperm meet. A literal light spark can be seen from the egg when fertilization happens.

I have often wondered about the use of force during conception and fear that the woman might become a binding agent of generational trauma to the embryo's genetic makeup as it forms into a baby.

Both men and women are disconnected from experiencing the healing of self-reliance monetarily and sexual recovery from positive sexual experiences through connection with their spouse. Self-healing and healing as a couple are possible through positive sexual experiences. This is a union of male and female energy into restructuring energy bodies or chakras for body healing.

I think about the way that Jesus elevated all of the women in his life and how he advocated for them. The image of Mary Magdalene comes to my mind.

Puritan culture is a branch of patriarchy. Puritan culture supports that a woman's inherent worth revolves around the intact virginity before the marriage. You would think that this ideal would make men more protective of innocence. Still, I often wonder if it causes the shame behind slut-shaming women who had sex before marriage, women who have children from different fathers, and disrespect from a husband to a wife once he knows she is no longer a virgin. Because men believe that a penis can change who a woman is, they treat her as soiled or easily discardable once virginity is no longer her reality.

This idea manifests as a Madonna-whore complex within marriages wherein the wife must stay a pristine Madonna. The sexual energy gets funneled toward the archetype of "whore," which looks like sex addictions, porn addictions, and infidelity. They exclude the wife from being the desire of the husband, cause a lack of deep connection between the couple, and stifle the woman's sexual pleasure toward her husband.

The dynamics of sex addictions within marriage are destructive for so many reasons. As much as the demonization of the person pursuing sex addiction is rampant in the blame game, it is most damaging to the soul of the person engaging in it. Sex addiction reduces the individual to nothing more than a gender incapable of controlling sexual impulses instead of encouraging the capacity to make capable and protective sexual decisions toward the betterment of marital intimacy.

Worldly patriarchal narratives are damaging in regards to finances too. What happens if a man loses his job, is injured in a way he cannot perform his job, or passes away? What happens to the man if he is struggling and the woman has so much of a "white knight" view of him that she is unyielding to his need to be supported in his struggle? The woman needs to be skilled at producing monetary abundance for the family without fearing how a husband may react.

As women, are we allowing space to accept these human men in their struggles or are we creating harsh environments with our expectations that our men cannot ever fail? Are we expecting men to die on their white horses before we accept them falling off of the horse and needing help back up?

Outliers, mavericks, and women who are "different" have been murdered so often throughout history that herd mentality became a necessity for women's survival. What would happen if we all recognized each other as sovereign beings with independent purposes in our marriages? What would happen in our church if we aligned toward a common goal? Do we even know what that goal is right now? Would positive, healthy sex between partners cause a radical shift in the miracles they bring to earth together?

Sovereignty in the form of alignment and safety of full expression helps the energy centers of our bodies align and work in our favor. The power of God is received into our crown chakra and flows through all of our other chakras.

Therefore, having control of our thoughts and our mind is more than just basic principles of discipline. It is the river through which priesthood power can flow through us so we can exercise it. If two individuals' souls, tied with a sealing ordinance, were able to experience power together instead of power "over," can you imagine how restorative that could be?

Control, fear, and the worldly patriarchy are man-made and aren't of God's energy, love, or true power. If control is the spark, then fear is the gasoline. Fear is a manufactured illusion that magnifies assumption into manipulation as an action. Fear creates the emotional binding agent that creates neural pathways of difficulty—deeper neural caverns of doubt block momentum toward faith in action.

Acting from fear comes from a belief that we are separate from God. Separation from God is a lie. We are always energetically connected to Him and to every living being on the planet. The collective energetic output from everyone on earth is collective consciousness.

An excellent book on interconnectedness is *You Are the Universe* by Deepak Chopra, M.D., and Menas Kafatos, Ph. D.

Humans share the capability to co-create with our Heavenly Parents. We too can organize matter into something new. Our bodies do this constantly when we heal from wounds, sickness, and traumatic emotions. We take one thing and turn it into something else. This is also called transmutation.

Any time we are engulfed in fear-mongering tactics to shut down someone else's autonomy, voice, or way of practicing belief, we mock God and rebuke our birthright.

Everything a person has to give back to God in the way they understand through the Holy Spirit is their right. The adversary loves to manipulate us through ego-driven thought processes. One way we create division out of fear-based ego is to look at how another human worships and cast stones at them, take away their temple recommends, and disfellowship them. By damning another for how they express their love for Divine Source, we deny our God. We cease to see or hear the truth in their worship. This unacceptance of anything outside of what we see fit is the act of a Pharisee. Never underestimate a widow's mite.

Shutting down to anything outside of the way that we think and believe is called "cognitive dissonance." Let me be upfront with you. You cannot be a part of the LDS religion, whose whole ideology revolves around the access of eternal soul binding, family lineage, and various practices of mysticism (to include receiving revelation), while not honoring the truths in the ancient ways like in earthbound religion.

Our ancestors witnessed the miracles of the earth before other people claimed their land to erect cities. They witnessed miracles before science jabbed the best guess of why they happened. They believed in our Heavenly Mother before politicians started claiming rights over their bodies and souls through murder and waves of forced conversion.

The "occult" campaign era of worldly patriarchy, which resulted in thousands of women murdered in witch trials, is to blame for the perversion and ambiguity of our Heavenly Mother to this day. At energetic origins, I see paganism and Christianity as two sides of the same divine energy coin: divine feminine and divine masculine.

FULL USE OF PRIESTHOOD POWER TOWARD RESTORATION

I've learned a lot about myself simply by studying other people with my personality type. Albert Einstein revolutionized physics with his discovery of the theory of general relativity. Random fact about me, I share a Myers-Briggs personality type with Einstein— INTP.

I am sure you already know about Einstein and his discovery. But what you may not know is that he needed the help of mathematicians to come up with the equation which represented his discovery.

In *You Are the Universe*, Chopra and Kafatos write, "Einstein could see in his mind's eye that objects would not appear to travel at the same speed to someone riding a beam of light and to someone standing on another moving object. Since the speed of anything is measured by the time it takes to travel a certain distance, suddenly time and space had to be relative as well. Very soon, Einstein's chain of reasoning became complicated—it took ten years, from 1905 to 1915, for him to consult mathematicians in order to find the correct formulation of his theory. In the end, the General Theory of Relativity was hailed as the greatest piece of science ever accomplished by a single mind. But it mustn't be lost that Einstein cracked the code of space, time, matter, energy, and gravity by using the experience of visual images."

$E = mc2$ is the mathematical equation that Einstein and mathematicians came up with to represent his theory properly. Simply put, it means that energy is THE SAME AS matter.

If energy is the same as matter, could this also be the basis with which we channel God's energy through our physical bodies? Einstein's discovery caused a warpath of nuclear explosions. Why couldn't it be a component for understanding how we exercise priesthood power or how we can heal the physical body with faith, belief, and meditation? I am not a physicist, so maybe I need some more education, but that is how my mind works.

Jesus Christ, who was the greatest metaphysician on the planet, showed us by example how we can activate the energy centers of our body to align with God and become a vessel of healing through the raw forces of our mind. This would also make Jesus and the Apostle Paul physicists who proved, long before scientific measurement methods were available, what we have access to in this life.

I believe that resurrection is a puzzle piece in Christ's teachings of overcoming physical ailment, with death becoming an initiation to more priesthood power. It is another unique principle of the LDS religion that may be worth pondering when considering the mystery of ancestors or spirits becoming visible to human beings.

Merkaba is mentioned in the Bible and can be translated to "chariot," or the literal vehicle of light that surrounds our body when our chakras are clear and in alignment. This is our vehicle to God in this life. The upward-facing pyramid shape in the Merkaba represents the divine masculine energy with the elements of air and fire. The downward-facing pyramid represents the divine feminine energy of water and earth elements. This chariot of God is activated by using our bodies with a regulated nervous system to receive personal revelation. In order to do this, we must have balanced male and female energies within our own bodies.

To fulfill the plan of salvation, we have to have all priesthood holders operating at their most total capacity. Male and female.

The safety provided to us as women toward panoptic potential and bold action is what male members of the Church can help us with. Worldly patriarchy still shackles us from standing in our full stature. We need men to defend and hold space. The 2021 movie *Dune* says it best with the line, "Fear is a mind-killer."

Women at their best are sustainers to their male counterparts and men, at their best, are safe containers of empowerment for their female counterparts to grow and rise in. Both male and female members of marriage must recognize each other as sovereign beings with individual soul paths to have a healthy relationship dynamic.

To actualize our priesthood power potential as individuals and as a couple, mental reframing exercises around commonly accepted definitions within areas exhibiting toxic culture would be beneficial. A major reframe needs to happen.

The High Priestess

THE PRIESTHOOD POWER OF WOMEN

WE ARE THE PROPHECY FULFILLED

WHAT DOES IT MEAN FOR WOMEN TO HAVE PRIESTHOOD POWER?

From a talk by Pres. Russell M. Nelson, entitled "A Plea to my Sisters:"

"Sisters, do you realize the breadth and scope of your influence when you speak those things that come to your heart and mind as directed by the Spirit? A superb stake president told me of a stake council meeting in which they were wrestling with a difficult challenge. At one point, he realized that the stake Primary president had not spoken, so he asked if she had any impressions. 'Well, actually I have,' she said and then proceeded to share a thought that changed the entire direction of the meeting. The stake president continued, 'As she spoke, the Spirit testified to me that she had given voice to the revelation we had been seeking as a council.'

"My dear sisters, whatever your calling, whatever your circumstances, we need your impressions, your insights, and your inspiration. We need you to speak up and speak out in ward and stake councils. We need each married sister to speak as 'a *contributing* and *full* partner' as you unite with your husband in governing your family. Married or single, you sisters possess distinctive capabilities and special intuition you have received as gifts from God. We brethren cannot duplicate your unique influence.

"We know that the culminating act of all creation was the creation of woman! We need your strength!

"Attacks against the Church, its doctrine, and our way of life are going to increase. Because of this, we need women who have a bedrock understanding of the doctrine of Christ and who will use that understanding to teach and help raise a sin-resistant generation. We need women who can detect deception in all of its forms. We need women who know how to access the power that God makes available to covenant keepers and who express their beliefs with confidence and charity. We need women who have the courage and vision of our Mother Eve.

"My dear sisters, nothing is more crucial to your eternal life than your own conversion. It is converted, covenant-keeping women—women like my dear wife Wendy—whose righteous lives will increasingly stand out in a deteriorating world and who will thus be seen as different and distinct in the *happiest* of ways.

"So today I plead with my sisters of The Church of Jesus Christ of Latter-day Saints to step forward! Take your rightful and needful place in your home, in your community, and in the kingdom of God—more than you ever have before. I plead with you to fulfill President Kimball's prophecy. And I promise you in the name of Jesus Christ that as you do so, the Holy Ghost will magnify your influence in an unprecedented way!"

I invite you to listen to the talk I quoted above in its entirety. You can do so by accessing it on YouTube or on churchofjesuschrist.org. I am the proof of a prophecy fulfilled in the latter days. I am one of them*, and so are you.*

You matter to this Church, you matter to our prophet, you are seen by our Heavenly Parents, and I need you to help me hold the line. I have exercised my priesthood power by being wholly obedient and, at times, by my defiance to enact change.

So, how have I exercised my priesthood power? Or, to reframe the question, how have I exercised access to God's power to be unapologetic?

Here are a few ways I've utilized my access to God's power:

- Speaking up and out about healing, boundaries, and change
- Facilitating hard conversations toward resolution
- Following promptings of the Holy Spirit
- Temple experiences
- Relief Society attendance
- Denying my calling or deciding NOT to go to church when injurious behavior of my ward threatened my family
- Protecting my family according to the dictates of my own sovereignty and personal relationship with God. Protection of the family is central to all Church teachings.

Heavenly Mother is the epitome of female priesthood power. I would add that Heavenly Mother, represented in the Bible with the Hebrew word "Shekhinah," is currently physically manifesting to the female members of the Church. Her visions and revelations from female members are needed to continue bringing prophesy into reality.

I have seen visions of Heavenly Mother since receiving my endowments in the Meridian, Idaho temple in October of 2020.

In regards to temples and prophets, I thought it was interesting to learn more about Solomon's temple from the Bible. When I was praying about writing this book, Heavenly Mother dropped in whispers of Solomon and prophets possessing the "keys" of priesthood power of both women and men. I read about Solomon. I felt through the Spirit that he was endowed with the priesthood power of holding space and logical wisdom. I also experienced a wave of knowledge that he also possessed a woman's intuition. I have had similar feelings about President Russell M. Nelson, Joseph Smith, and Gordon B. Hinckley.

THE CHURCH:
FROM SCARCITY TO ABUNDANCE

My livelihood is within the realm of taking creative and spiritual entrepreneurs from mindsets of scarcity to abundance in their business through utilizing personal life stories to create clear brand messaging. Clear messaging enables entrepreneurs to appeal to their ideal clients and magnetize money-making opportunities through the law of vibration.

One of the most colossal struggles my clients face at the beginning of our work together is the shift from a scarcity mindset to an abundance mindset. During the transition from scarcity to abundance, the growth phase feels almost like death. It is the end of the old self and dysfunctional ideologies to shift into claiming what is rightfully ours, i.e., a birthright of abundance.

When raising the energetic vibration of the mindset, life circumstances show similar death phases. Anything not aligned with the new, higher vibrations of the abundance mindset will fall away from the individual's life. This will look like the loss of friends, the loss of a 9 to 5 job, and maybe a divorce, breakup, or relationship problems. This part of the growth phase looks like destruction, much like a seed's process when sprouting a tiny plant from its shell. The source must be destroyed by the expanding growth of the plant to allow for new life to spring forth.

Clients will often panic during this phase and start questioning everything we have established up to that point. I believe that a part of the ego and old narratives must die at this point of the growth phase if the new abundance of growth will survive and take root to expand further. Faith as a function of propelling desired outcomes upward has a make it or break it component to actualizing potential.

As I have dissected my experiences and the culture of the Church, I have seen a similar pattern. The Church is currently in the thralls of immense growing pains. The Church making decisions in scarcity mode is a past narrative.

I see the scarcity phase of the Church as the very planting of the Church into the soil of the earth when Joseph Smith saw his first vision. The pioneers were losing their lives in early history. They were chased out of cities. They migrated across the country at significant risk to themselves and their children simply to plant the Church. Part of the gender-specific narratives, such as "the wife stays home while the man goes out and makes money" was necessary to maintain the worldly cultural normalcy of the times when women had no rights to vote or be heard.

This particular structure still maintained within a progressive church is far behind the times. Can we continue to hemorrhage female members in modern-day Zion because of a rigidity that leaves women feeling unsafe to be who they were made to be? Are we going to continue to put all the pressure on blended families to restore what didn't need to be broken in the first place? Or are we going to get to the root causes and get rid of the dysfunction?

Our Heavenly Mother is done with not being an active participant in the narrative of the Church. I do not adhere to the belief that my Heavenly Father wants to "protect" Her from being slandered. That's why we aren't talking about Her? I'm not buying that She would passively stand by, watching Her daughters burn at the hands of Her sons for Her own protection. She is speaking and appearing to the women of the Church that are awakening. I have felt Her rage as Sunday lessons about Biblical stories do not include Her.

I do not subscribe to the narrative that my Father desires and expects a silent wife that He speaks for. She is His equal and is capable of speaking for Herself. She is now awakening and speaking through many female members of the Church. The refusal of male leadership to acknowledge the unique priesthood capabilities given to women by adherence to our covenants and understanding Heavenly Mother pushes many female members out of the Church. They're going into the wilderness, wounded.

Now that the Church has taken root and is established, these old narratives leave many female members of the Church feeling like they don't have a place in the Church. Female priesthood power is more than the relational dynamics we have been taught is our only area of impact. Sadly, families are now being torn apart as the vibrational energy of women actualizing their priesthood power rises and male priesthood holders are proving unsafe for us.

The lower vibrational energy within marriage is causing too much of a separation between spouses. Instead of males being empowered to rise up to meet our vibrations, the opposite is happening. The female is being shamed, blamed, or degraded into lowering her vibrations to match his. This expectation of female priesthood holders to remain small is unacceptable because it prevents the entire family's spiritual progression as they are soul-tied together.

Soul work that is not accomplished in this life by a soul will be required after the death of the physical body. We should be promoting learning from and rising to the highest vibration found within each family unit. Then cultivating for growth to the next level.

The irony is that female power in the energetic space is perfect for balancing the unchecked male ego and unrighteous dominion when in alignment. Males are in dire need of having more checks and balances in place to ensure safe leadership at all levels within the Church structure. Unchecked male power is a commonality that keeps coming up when I speak to women who have left the Church. If several women have the same shared experience, we must adjust to provide better systems.

So many women were asked inappropriate questions during bishop interviews as adolescents, their husbands' sexual sins were dismissed as minimal problems, and they were blatantly gaslighted by leaders about the abuse they endured. Do you think that if a leader's wife or a female elder of the Church community was sitting in the room during those experiences those things would have happened? Possibly, but it's less likely.

I am unsettled that once a male priesthood holder holds a title of influence within the Church on any level, he is never questioned. These are still human males (predominantly Caucasian in my geographical location) who are conditioned by their lived experience, cultural and generational upbringing, and who still need systems of accountability to not abuse positions of power given by other male leaders.

You would probably not even believe how many fallible male leaders of this Church have pushed female members to leave due to their unchecked actions. I will be as bold as to say that not allowing more space for female priesthood power to be understood, exercised, and implemented aggravates the injustices we have faced and pushes us toward aggression. The top tier of leadership in the Church of Jesus Christ of Latter-day Saints would do well to provide space, time, and an invitation to hear the stories of the women who have left or want to leave the Church due to a male priesthood holder's actions. These heartbreaking stories should be the basis of how Church systems of checks and balances are put into place to avoid abuse of power over future generations.

This leads me to demand more from male priesthood holders in the way of holding space for female priesthood power by developing ways we can express our experiences in safe settings.

There also needs to be systems for appropriate checks and balances during interviews about specific topics with our female members. Support systems need to be developed where restoration of the family unit IS possible, i.e., the blended family.

As systems are developed for better accountability and safety provisions for female members of the Church, assumptions shouldn't be made about what they need to feel safe. ASK THEM SPECIFICALLY. When it comes to revelations on Heavenly Mother and what it means to be a woman exercising Priesthood Power, STOP ASKING MEN; ask the female members of the Church.

Female voices and revelations on the topics need to be allowed to free flow out of the women who are priesthood holders within the Church. I am hearing a lack of tolerance with women that sounds like: We will no longer deny our silent Mother. We will not abandon our children. Church attendance and membership will be the first to go if we are forced to make these choices of dismembering our families and sacred relationship with Mother.

Once the damage control of how things have been failing is managed appropriately, I believe the Church will experience a flourishing growth period. If the Church is the Bride of Christ, then, in that context, a bride has different needs as she matures in a marriage.

Men are holding offices in the patriarchal order of the church structure because they are a masculine energetic structure that holds space for women to be safe to exercise priesthood power. But there is not much out there to explain women and the priesthood.

Heavy questions weighed on my shoulders while researching for this book. Those questions look like:

- What are the roles of masculine energy vs. feminine energy?
- Are there specific gifts that men and women are naturally better at?
- What is the best balance of healthy masculine and feminine energy within one person?
- Once that balance is reached, what is the best pairing of masculine and feminine in a human coupling?

In-depth education on learning individual skills, spiritual gifts, personality strengths, and the true meaning of priesthood power would give more direction to all church members.

ADVERSARY WEAPON IDENTIFICATION
CHURCH CULTURAL PROBLEMS WITHIN MODERN DAY "ZION"

"These six things doth the Lord hate: yea, seven are an
abomination unto him: A proud look, a lying tongue, and
hands that shed innocent blood, An heart that deviseth
wicked imaginations, feet that be swift in running to
mischief, A false witness that speaketh lies, and he that
soweth discord among brethren."
(Proverbs 6:16-19 KJV)

THE LIE OF SEPARATION FROM GOD IS A WEAPON IN THE ARSENAL OF THE ADVERSARY

I feel prompted to lean into the false idea that we can ever be
separated from God. This thought is a fear-based illusion. Whatever
we are creating in our life is a result of the way that we are using our
imagination. If I am focused on imagining all the negative things
that could happen, I am training my mind to release cortisol (a stress
hormone) and see the bad as I go through my day-to-day life. The
human body was hardwired to respond to threats and fight back
against predators and life-threatening encounters.

When something or someone crosses your path that your brain
perceives as a threat, the hypothalamus responds with an alarm to
the body. The hypothalamus signals the kidneys through nerves and

hormones to release cortisol and adrenaline. The negative mind becomes a broken switch that tells our body that we are constantly under attack.

The adrenaline released will increase heart rate, elevate blood pressure, and boost energy supplies. Cortisol will elevate blood sugar (or glucose) in the bloodstream and suppress the digestive, reproductive, and growth processes.

All of the cultural separation, the terms we use to label, and the shame we take out of the toolbox to segregate are just various lies that create the distorted thinking patterns that we are distant from God. God is in all of our bodies—our God is in the coding of our DNA on cellular levels. Any time that an illusion of separation is perpetuated within the Church body, the adversary has infiltrated. (Connections made from the book *When She Was Bad: Violent Women and the Myth of Innocence* by Patricia Pearson.)

Let's start with the weapons in the armory of the adversary. The aspects of toxic church culture that I identify in this book are the adversary's weapons of division and exclusion.

I have witnessed a massive divide between LDS doctrine and principles from the culture of the Church that its members have adopted over time. Since I joined the Church, I have not had issues with the male authorities or male members. I know this is not everyone's experience, so I speak from my own. My experiences are suitable catalysts that built my momentum toward writing this book.

When actions start feeling energetically familiar to me, and my hackles go up, I know we have a problem. The world is too enmeshed in church culture right now. I see it plainly because I was once a creature devoted to the world.

I have some unique experiences that will be highlighted in this book because they are relevant to a current family dynamic in the Church, namely, the blended family. Current divorce rates in the Church of Jesus Christ of Latter-day Saints are roughly equal to secular rates of divorce. The blended family has become a typical result of the divorce rates. Currently, there are zero resources for blended family dynamics within LDS church guides, bishop handbooks, etc.

The way blended families are viewed saddens me. The new marriage and the blended family dynamic are often seen as a consolation prize rather than a vital source of renewal for broken hearts. This view and upholding of the "first wife" or "previous spouse" with entitled and inappropriate rights by extended family or ward members can contribute to continued marital failure within the current marriage. Frankly, it is a form of emotional polygamy that is unfair to the current spouse.

My blended family and I have mostly suffered from the injurious behaviors of the female members of the Church of Jesus Christ of Latter-day Saints in my geographical area. I want to shed light on the information that has come to me about church culture vs. the Church at its core. I will provide examples of my personal experiences with toxic church culture and what I have observed in my ward regarding my blended family dynamic. No, I do not take the stance that the whole church is rotten simply because of my experience with some people in the Church being negative. I do not reject God because of the actions of fallible people. I have still developed friendships with female members of the Church, but the injurious behavior of others has caused enough damage to my marriage and family that I need to bring it up. I am sure we are not an isolated incident.

Divorce can be a weapon of the adversary because the separation of a family unit drives scarcity and survival and keeps solo parents scrambling. If we are too focused on survival, we cannot build a spiritual or an earthly legacy. I am not asserting divorce is a weapon in cases of abuse, addiction, or any other form of neglect within a marriage. Divorce can have restorative qualities for an individual in extreme situations. My efforts are pouring into the blended family dynamic and not breaking what doesn't need to be broken.

I love this Church and I love God. If anything, my negative experiences have helped me to empathize with the rejection my Savior faced. In some capacity, rejection is a part of following Christ on His same path. If Jesus is to be the company I keep energetically, I am happy to be rejected.

I am using my real-life examples so you can understand how the damage of injurious behaviors can bleed out from unrighteous dominion and cause long-term harm to a member's personal life. Detrimental behaviors from ward members can even become legal issues for a member of the Church. These acts can magnify feelings of rejection and isolation that a member may already feel through a divorce, ultimately pushing that individual away from the Church.

These are my real-life experiences with unrighteous dominion exercised over my husband, family, or me under a "church calling" by women inhabiting predominantly relational roles within the Church.

About a month after my current husband, Mike, divorced his ex-wife, she decided to move out of the joint residence they had shared during the last few years of their marriage. Mike was at work while several ward members came to his home and moved property out of the house. Some members who helped clear the residence were also in attendance at a public event where Mike's ex-wife spoke poorly of him on a stage in front of his oldest child. Mike came home to an emptied house. At no time did any of the members request to see a divorce decree from Mike, which typically spells out legal property division by the judge presiding over the civil case.

The following Sunday, Mike was getting his children ready for church and could not find baby blankets or some of the kids' personal belongings that were supposed to be in the house. Upset,

Mike still managed to make it to church and had to sit with members of his "ward family," who had emptied his home of belongings just days prior. Mike remained in the ward assigned to his physical residence. In this incident, all ward members involved in helping his ex-wife move out of the home without considering the legal decree were potentially liable for a lawsuit. They had engaged in moving property they had not specified was assigned to a specific party in the divorce and damaged their relationship with Mike.

I had enough of the participation of our ward members in several violations of a joint custody agreement between Mike and his ex-wife. The knee-jerk response I received was, "We were just doing our duty as Christians to be nice to her, and that's what Jesus would want" or "They're her kids too."

In the book *When She Was Bad: Violent Women and the Myth of Innocence*, Patricia Pearson writes, "In monogamous primates, loyalty was imposed by the females, not the males." She also states, "The basic dynamics of the mating system depend on the degree to which one female tolerates another." She goes on to discuss that any time there is a prospect of a male having multiple mates, there is a fierce antagonism by the females of breeding age toward each other.

I have met with my bishop several times about the issues we have faced as a blended family. There are currently no sections in the handbook regarding properly handling or educating members on legal liabilities when violating aspects of a blended family dynamic. There are also no support mechanisms in place for blended families. This concerns me because, statistically, every subsequent marriage to the first marriage has a higher divorce rate.

I believe that blended families are not treated well within the current culture of the LDS church by other women because it is construed as a competition. In particular, I have felt that women have seen me as a threat to the limiting beliefs that keep them exercising unrighteous dominion over other women in the Church. Church "events" and primary programs are a new battleground for ward members to incite drama by stepping out of bounds to invite an ex-spouse without the custodial parent's knowledge. Regardless of a sign on a church building that says, "Visitors Welcome," legal custodial agreements can be broken when ward members overstep these agreements.

Out of sheer curiosity, I contacted a couple of members in different countries to ask them questions about their experience with church culture. None of the individuals I spoke with had seen the same thing where they live and go to church. I then asked members of the Idaho, Arizona, and Utah areas about the culture of the Church. They all had the same or similar experiences to my own. I found this fascinating. Has modern-day "Zion" become a Pharisee podium of judgment from which members self-righteously choose who is worthy of acceptance and who gets cast out?

WEAPON OF THE ADVERSARY TACTIC 1: THE DAMAGE OF GENERALIZING FEMALE PRIESTHOOD AUTHORITY, NEUROSCIENCE, AND IMPACTS OF SOCIAL MEDIA

When I asked the two young missionaries helping me prepare for my endowments what it meant for women to have priesthood power, they were not able to answer this question in its entirety.

They humbly responded that they weren't entirely sure what it meant. Their best guess was that female priesthood power must do with women's work within their families and church callings.

Generalizing the power of the priesthood as it pertains to women and defining it only through the context of church callings and their ability within families reduces women to maintaining only a relational universe in their dynamics with men and children. These limitations are forms of sexism rooted in untruths and half-truths

40

about the capacity of women. The Church is structured in a patriarchal way, but should not be confused with how we think of patriarchy as an oppressive structure of the world to exercise unrighteous dominion.

Until recently, women have been assumed to be incapable of violence even though women are the central gender committing infanticide. According to research cited in *When She Was Bad: Violent Women and the Myth of Innocence* by Patricia Pearson, women who are allowed a say-so in the patriarchal structures that keep them locked in a relational universe tend to exert control through injurious behaviors. Researchers consider injurious behaviors such as rejection, isolation, instigation of violence, and methods of self-harm equally as damaging as the outward physical violence displayed by their male counterparts.

The sexism of researchers has kept female behavior a mystery. An excellent example of this is how I went through most of my life undiagnosed even though I am a "high functioning" individual on the spectrum for autism. I don't like being called high functioning simply because I am a type of neurodivergent that can mimic "normal" behavior enough to "blend in." There were no tests to measure women on the spectrum because girls and women have been tested based on male displays of autism until recently. You will find similar issues of women receiving improper diagnoses because of male-developed testing in other types of neurodivergence such as ADHD. I don't even like calling anything I have experienced a "disorder" because I do not believe how I see, think, or feel is a "disorder." I should not have to conform to make other people comfortable. I should not have to cause pain to myself to learn or do things the way everyone else does.

I found it difficult to find studies on female violence outside of correctional settings analyzing female inmates and factors contributing to violent offenses. However, I did come across scientific data about how the brain processes rejection and isolation. The term "injurious behavior" is valid because when an individual is isolated or rejected by a class or group member, the brain registers that rejection or isolation the same way it registers physical injury. Mental anguish impacts the body and the spirit. If you learn only one truth from what I am writing, I hope that it is the truth of how interconnected the mind, body, and soul are with one another.

An article entitled "A Quantitative Meta-Analysis of Functional Imaging Studies of Social Rejection" states: "Various cultures and languages use terms and phrases for physical pain (e.g., hurt, searing, broken heart) to describe social rejection, but is the similarity between a nociceptive physical stimulus and social rejection literal or figurative? There is a surprisingly large behavioral literature suggesting that the similarity may be literal. The addition of the neuroimaging evidence showing that social rejection activates the pain matrix seemed to make an overwhelming case for social rejection coopting the physical pain system in humans" (Cacioppo, S., et al, 2013).

Another study was conducted by researchers interested in the impact of targeted social rejection in an online platform designed to simulate social media. The researchers found that the female who was rejected in an online environment was less willing to cooperate with the "mean girls" in a real-life activity after social rejection had occurred online. The aggression of the rejected female and the desire to retaliate against those targeting her increased. (Radke, S., et al, 2021).

Let's go back to my previous statement about the generalization of female priesthood power and reframe it, keeping in mind the new information that we just learned. The problem with generalizing female power of the priesthood and limiting it only to church callings and familial duties within a patriarchal societal religion is that:

1. It can quickly get twisted into unrighteous dominion labeled as "permission" from men (in this case, male church leaders) for women to unleash a type of psychological aggression or warfare on other members of the Church.

2. An unrighteous and abusive female hierarchy develops and decides whether another member of the Church is deemed "unworthy." The body of the targeted member takes this injurious behavior the same way as physical pain.

I am curious what the suicide and suicide attempt statistics are within the female population of the Church. This toxic dynamic within imbalanced Relief Societies and extended family female dynamics within church culture likely contribute to depression and suicidal ideation. Mental health could be significantly improved by giving women the freedom to explore and express what access to priesthood power means for them.

Similarly, female members speaking about their revelations of our Heavenly Mother would strengthen and empower every member of this church. I do not believe it is a male priesthood holder's right to tell a woman what she already knows to be true about her divine Mother. As in the earthly dynamics of mother-daughter relations, a female child will receive more instruction from her mother when she needs guidance throughout her life as she reaches adolescence and adulthood. A man cannot teach a woman how to be a woman.

From my understanding, transgender isn't a recognized gender by the Church hierarchy. If this is the case, I do not see how cross-gender instruction toward my role as a human female can be given by a male. Something must concede as there is no need for a foot in the mouth and words not matching behavior within the leadership of the Church. People within and without the Church are angry about the lack of inclusion of people from the LGTBQIA2S+ community, but let's be honest—women are still not recognized as sovereign beings who receive revelation worth being spoken into existence, and this is an identified gender by the Church. Women are the sole reason families are even an option on the earth. Family is the core lifeforce of why this Church is in existence. Help us help you here.

A study on the relationship between social rejection and depression states, "Social rejection events greatly increase risk for depression. They also appear to bring about depression more quickly than non-rejection events. For example, Slavich and colleagues examined the effects of a specific type of rejection called targeted rejection (TR), which involves the exclusive, active, and intentional rejection of an individual by others. Individuals who experienced a recent severe TR event became depressed approximately three times faster than those who experienced a severe life event that was not defined as TR. Again, because these events were all rated severe using a state-of-the-art, interview-based measure of stress, the relatively quicker onset of depression following TR is likely due to the specific characteristics that define TR events, as opposed to differences in the severity of TR versus non-TR life events" (Slavich, et al., 2009).

Another issue with keeping education limited to the actual authority and ignoring the revelations of women who hold priesthood power is that it keeps us suppressed from claiming rites of passage necessary for the next level of spiritual progression. The denial of female power is holding every priesthood holder back from progressing.

One of these rites of passage of spiritual progression of women is the rite of abundance in our financial capabilities. The ability to produce financial abundance appears to be a natural byproduct of women aligned with their soul's purpose.

Barbara Huson, an expert on women and wealth, beautifully explains this concept in her book *Sacred Success: A Course in*

Financial Miracles. Spirituality has the potential to elevate all areas of our lives, whether physically or metaphysically. I highly recommend Barbara Huson's book if you are a woman who is ready to transition from financial dependence to being an independent provider. Huson addresses what she calls "metafiscal" processes, including inviting God into your relationship with money to break through money blocks and receive abundance.

I love what Huson said in *Sacred Success* about the possibility of a healthy union of males and females shifting old-world narratives and paradigms. She asserts, "I predict that as the tenets of Sacred Success become more widely known and practiced, we'll see women's levels of influence soar exponentially. And because of women's increasing impact, in partnership with enlightened men, it will be fascinating to watch how the global climate shifts."

TRADITIONAL GENDER ROLES AND THE BLENDED FAMILY "LIABILITY"

Gender doesn't dictate that a specific sex will be good at something. I operate outside the norms of traditional nuclear family roles with my current spouse. My husband stays home and runs all things kid-related in our blended family of eight kids. He is better at that than I am. On the other hand, I make money in an untraditional, hybrid business model as a luxury brand consultant and traveling photographer.

That's what works for our family. If I bought into the idea that I have to be a prototype of a woman as defined by outside standards, I would very simply not want to be alive anymore. To constantly feel external pressure that you are not "good enough" for what you're supposed to be best at is a special kind of hell we all need to evolve past.

I had an epiphany in February of 2021 when I set out to find the truth about my identity as a daughter of Heavenly Parents. I started with unbiased sources. I took a Myers-Briggs personality type test, and I discovered my Human Design Type, enneagram, and Clifton Strengths Finders. There was a moment in my home office where I sat in the surreal truth that everything I held in my hand from Clifton Strengths Finders said my strengths were the same things I had been told I was "BAD" for. I began ruthlessly editing my life from that point forward. I cut ties with people who were not bringing me peace. I stopped reacting to antagonists. I started restructuring my life around what I was best at. The best part of this personal knowledge was remaining sovereign in my internal climate when the outside world tried to imprint chaos into me. When the adversary used other people to try to wear me down, I was able to stand firm in my truth and say, "I do not agree to that. That is not who I am. I am actually really great at _____."

Much could be learned about the restructuring of the Church to function at its highest capabilities if we knew more about each member's personal strengths. Depression, injurious behaviors, and broken relationships would not be as prevalent if we could mirror strength back to each member of the Church. Once these individual strengths are identified, we would be able to assign church callings and set the Church up for rapid growth. The Church can experience growth faster by playing to the stability of each individual.

Right now, callings feel like a shot in the dark method of randomly assigning callings and trying to develop weaknesses with these callings. Members would be living in alignment with their purpose on earth with this initiative.

Jessica Tietjen, an expert on cultivating peak performance in workplaces, homes, and communities, utilizes CliftonStrengths in her work and asserts in her book, *The Exceptional Life R-Evolution*, "I have performed numerous sessions with hundreds of people on strengths and seen the impact that learning your strengths can have on your relationships, results, and life. After six years of applying the insights from my strengths to my work and personal life, I know the benefits can be life-altering. By understanding who we are and what comes naturally, we can focus on our talents and turn them into strengths where we can occasionally achieve near-perfect performance. And who wouldn't want to strive for near-perfect performance?"

She goes on to state, "Our talents form the foundation for reaching peak performance. Fully knowing ourselves and our talents provides us the greatest opportunity to reach peak performance in all the roles we perform. Our strengths or talents can get us started (and are certainly the best way to get started) on the journey of self-awareness. Still, we must also consider additional components of who we are and our personal capabilities."

My blended family structure and non-traditional roles of man and woman in leadership roles of that family leave me feeling empathy for any member of the Church outside of the "norm." Anyone outside of what is culturally "acceptable" by the boss of the pecking order will feel like they do not have a place in the Church. Every maverick, every new pioneer, every convert, and every Benjamite might be too far of an outlier by the homogeneous standards of current culture to successfully gather the rest of scattered Israel if dynamics do not change. Every woman in the Church of Jesus Christ of Latter-day Saints deserves to find safety in their Relief Society. Women need a strong community of other supportive women.

This is a concept that I could logically wrap my mind around because it seems like it's a no-brainer. On the surface, you're thinking, "Of course, women need communities of other women! That's why the Relief Society was established."

But, in over thirty years of life, I had not experienced the transformative power of a loving community of women until I went to a retreat led by Keira Poulsen in Missouri. Keira is a successful

47

female entrepreneur who helps women receive the books they intend to write. She then holds space for the authors and helps them overcome any limitations to bring their book into physical form. While writing this book, I utilized her services, and I cannot even put words to the number of miracles I experienced during my time with Keira. I am forever grateful for her stepping into her calling because she has changed my life for the better.

The retreat attendees are all women tackling necessary topics of how they transmuted some form of personal life pain into higher consciousness. Each woman there held space as we healed individually and collectively. We recovered from wounds still present because we were able to be safe in our vulnerability of sharing our stories. As each woman was vulnerable, the other women supported her.

I faced many of my fears during this retreat, including an experience I had jumping into a freezing cold lake in Innsbrook, Missouri. The power of a community of like-minded and aligned women is healing. It's becoming creation doulas for the other women. A community of women in pure form looks like a united heart space force that brings the manifestation of miracles at a fast pace. We created an energetic "caravan" of chariots, speeding toward a new territory of quantum healing. At that authors' retreat, each of us aligned with the light of our own "Merkaba" (a term found in the Bible for the chariot of God). A Merkaba is sacred geometry from the origins of the Flower of Life.

Together, we became a spiritual light rail that sped up miraculous delivery for every one of us. The power of a group investing lifeforce toward the same goal was a powerful experience I needed.

Scientifically, group meditation creates synergy, and studies have found that healing happens on a larger scale when meditation occurs in a group setting rather than meditating alone. A ripple effect then occurs, resulting in peace in the environment and lives of the meditation participants.

Julio L. Matta asserts, "Recorded EEG results show that brainwaves synchronize while meditating. EEG stands for electroencephalogram, which is a test used to evaluate the electrical activity in the brain." This statement blew my mind. I had a vision at the retreat that I didn't understand was a part of this book until I had written the last paragraph. The vision is written in my journal, and I highlight it later in the book, but I will mention the beginning of my vision here as it is pertinent.

I asked God, "What is possible with this book that I don't know?" I saw and wrote down at the retreat: "The City of Enoch hovering above the ground. Then I saw us, a circle of 12 women levitated above the City. Then a bright star above us."

I am so grateful to God for my experience of witnessing the united love of a circle of women in action on the retreat. Several mother wounds were healed as they mothered me. I was able to see myself in a light I haven't before because of the reflections of love they mirrored to me. I love these sisters of mine and cherish the experience I didn't think was possible in the fellowship of other women.

As I previously addressed with the information about how feelings of rejection and isolation are registered in the brain, it is no wonder that we are seeing a mass exodus of members who are choosing to become inactive or leave the Church. Being a man and exposure to the male hierarchy of the Church as a man is not in my wheelhouse, so I cannot speak on that topic. I feel that an overall survey of how things are currently working for male members would be beneficial.

SOCIAL MEDIA AND REINFORCEMENT OF TARGETED SOCIAL REJECTION

Social media has become another avenue to push social isolation and deepen the physiological pain a member may be feeling from their "ward family," especially amongst the female gender. Exclusion or being kept separate from the group has negative impacts on the mind of the black sheep. Social media is not an exception and lends to reinforcing damaging behavior of the pecking order of toxic LDS female members.

I have experience with this specific dynamic in my ward. Two female members moderate a Facebook group where all members of my ward who are added can post neighborhood news and program announcements. While this is used for ward news, it is not an official group initiated by local church leadership.

The "friendly" Ustick Ward became an emotional war zone for a while for our ten-person blended family. After my husband's ex-wife moved out of the residence, relocated outside of the ward boundaries, petitioned for their sealing to be canceled, and left the Church, she was still permitted access to this Facebook group. This caused many problems. The joint custody agreement was breached several times because she could access all information about church programs happening during my husband's custodial time.

The group's moderators, both female members, refused to remove her from the group when I brought up the issues it was causing. One refused to answer me directly but sent the message through the other moderator that the ex-wife hadn't posted anything inappropriate, so she would not be removed from the group. Still, I could leave it if I disapproved of their decision.

I still feel uncomfortable that information about where my children will be is posted in a social media forum where all past and present members of the ward are able to view it. This information about youth should be reserved for a more private method of communication, like emailed directly to parents or placed in the ward bulletin that is handed out on Sundays.

I have had single members, members who struggle with infertility, and divorced members express similar feelings about shame around not fitting into a stereotypical family box because the LDS religion is centered around marriage and family. Shame is the lie that says we are bad for being who we are. It is the lie someone else told us that we agreed to believe. Any shame-inducing aspect of church culture needs to be scrubbed out with a wire brush.

Shame acts as a closing agent in our minds. An open mind is a crucial receptor for receiving God's power. Aligning the energy centers within our nervous systems in spaces of radical acceptance would cause a massive energy shift for the better and allow individuals to actualize their full potential on this earth and as members of the Church of Jesus Christ Latter-day Saints.

I am focusing on the body systems in this book because the body is a tool for exercising priesthood power to its fullest extent. When the nervous systems and energy centers are clear, we find a connection with Heavenly Mother. When the body's energy centers are clear and the human body is free from shame or fear influences, the nervous system reaches out like tree branches to receive the light of Christ. The reception of heavenly light into clear energy centers of the body creates the sacred chariot of light, or Merkaba, around the body—a vehicle for the human soul to transcend to God.

Heavenly Mother's dominion exists in the body. Heavenly Mother is in the systems and processes of how the body receives God. This is also in line with divine feminine energy (receptive, flowing, emotive). This personal revelation on Heavenly Mother became a witness to why the Word of Wisdom must be adhered to. The substances and acts associated with our side of covenant-keeping remove chemical addictions. Our nervous systems are pure enough to have somatic regulation within our bodies to experience

God as the Father and God as our Heavenly Mother. As my husband once said about caffeine, "It's great for ideas, bad for putting those ideas into action." The body can become a physiological and neurological hardwired container of unregulated states of addiction or sin that block channels to receive revelation and God's power.

I find it fascinating that I tripped upon the idea of women being a major block to women actualizing priesthood power potential. Women seem to be a significant problem, but the bright side of that coin is that women are also the solution. Women are keeping women small as individuals and also policing other women who are trying to grow into spiritual giantess levels. This female policing stems from the conditioning of worldly patriarchy and has no place in the restored Church of Jesus Christ.

This behavior may ironically double as a form of protection from the harsh discipline of the male hierarchy of the Church. It doesn't seem like feminists are looked upon with love and respect within church culture. That, however, is hypocrisy if we are also taught that women matter, families matter, and we have a Heavenly Mother.

I am not attempting to shame anyone with these insights. I simply want to educate so that people can know better than shrinking or harming others. Once we know there is better, it is our responsibility to do better.

Ambivalence about women's capabilities in alignment with correct usage of priesthood power revolves around the axis of claiming our abundance, transitioning through the essential phases of our lives that lead to spiritual progression. Abundance is our birthright, and frankly, it's God's side of the two-way agreement in covenant-making. Our responsibility is to strive and continually ask for the abundance owed to us. Anything or anyone that says otherwise is just noise and distraction.

WEAPON OF THE ADVERSARY TACTIC 2: DISMEMBERING THE FAMILY BODY WITH TERMINOLOGY LIKE "PART MEMBER" AND "NON-MEMBER"

There was a portion of time at the beginning of my current marriage when I was not a member of the Church. I supported my spouse with his religious beliefs and church attendance. I would go with him to Church sporadically and clung to terms used to describe my family, such as "part member family" or "non-member," when referring to my kids or me specifically. It felt isolating and separative to literally dismember families with mixed religious beliefs using terms like "part member" or "non-member." Now that I have been immersed in this religion for roughly three years, I have a new heartache for these terms.

Jesus taught us many things and one of them was the power of the words we speak. He used words to lasso energy from other dimensions and pull it through to this plane of existence. Words, combined with His access to the power of God, were the keys He used to unlock the mysteries of the universe and create miracles. He healed people on cellular levels and even brought back the dead to the land of the living. After being crucified and entombed for three days, he experienced this same resurrection of His own body. There is an element of priesthood power that increases in strength after the physical body dies.

James 1:26-27 says, "If anyone thinks he is religious and does not bridle his tongue but deceives his heart, this person's religion is worthless. Pure religion and undefiled before God and the Father is this, To visit the fatherless and widows in their affliction, and to keep himself unspotted from the world."

It would be wise to handle the family dynamic that is not a cookie-cutter LDS norm with some more sensitivity. These terms may be meant harmlessly at the level of intent, but they cause a feeling of division and exclusion to the person receiving these terms to describe their family. Why are we using these terms to dissect a family?

WEAPON OF THE ADVERSARY TACTIC 3: TOXIC CHURCH CULTURE AND MODERN-DAY POLYGAMY WITHIN THE BLENDED FAMILY DYNAMIC

We talked about early Church history in November 2021 with our kids, and we touched on the topic of polygamy. Something clicked inside me that correlated old church practices of polygamy to dysfunctional cultural expectations I have experienced firsthand toward the modern-day blended family.

LDS cultural standards (remember, not to be confused with the true Church) have adopted a modern form of polygamy regarding the blended family dynamic. I'd like to educate you on how that feels and how it's reinforced by a toxic church culture that's NOT in line with doctrine.

I am a convert to the Church and the third wife of a man raised in the Church. When I say "third wife," I mean that he was divorced from the other two before civilly marrying me. His former ex-wives have always had involvement in trash-talking me, trying to drive wedges in my marriage, etc. So, it feels similar to a pecking order dynamic of a polygamist family. Especially when his ex has said to my face that she still wants to have a sexual relationship with my husband.

My husband has kids with his second ex-wife. I have been scapegoated, manipulated, gaslit, and degraded by members of the Church telling me I had to allow his ex-wife to be involved in how my home runs. (Even with four other children I gave birth to in our home that are not involved with the ex at all). I've been told I should allow unlimited and unsupervised access by the ex to my husband.

The complete prejudice I have experienced as a new convert in my ward and by my in-laws has been a driving force behind why I've been ready to throw in the towel on my marriage. This psychological abuse has tempted me heavily to also leave the Church. These are super weird expectations of me because the entire religion, doctrine, and temple ordinances revolve around the importance of keeping a family unit together.

We decided not to attend Church as a family when the conflict between my husband and his ex-wife increased. There have been very brief periods when there was no high conflict between the parties. But we decided not to attend Church during those periods of heightened conflict because someone in my ward called me "sister" and invited a poisonous viper into my sacred space without asking us if we were okay with it. There is no regard for my feelings despite where I am with my husband or my family. It was sheer disrespect for the personal boundaries I vocalized in Relief Society after similar past incidents.

This behavior from my ward has left me feeling like I have not had a marriage with the man I share a last name with. It's been nearly impossible to have a new, thriving, and healthy relationship with so many people adding weight to the failure of its integrity.

Before becoming a member of the Church of Jesus Christ of Latter-day Saints, I believed in the eternal binding of souls or "soul ties." One of the hardships that blended families face is the temple sealing of the old spouse to the current spouse. I decided to wait until the sealing was canceled between my husband and his previous spouses before I would walk forward into that space with him.

There was no Church support group for the amount of hell that these experiences have been or their toll on my marriage.

The High Priestess

THE FUNCTION OF
RAGE TRANSMUTING
PAIN INTO POWER

"Some days I am more wolf than woman and
I am still learning how to stop apologizing for my wild."
- Nikita Gill

All emotions can serve a productive function if channeled into the right end goal. Harsh feelings also have a purpose of being transmuted into something else for better empathy, understanding, and personal growth. The key here is not to hang on to those difficult emotions for too long or they will settle in the body's tissues and cause disease. Extreme emotions have the potential also to destroy one's environment or relationships.

Rage has been an emotion that I have learned to turn into forward movement through some pretty grueling life experiences. I believe that women have a closer relationship and better understand what I am talking about than men. Female gender cultural treatment provides us ample opportunities to swallow our feelings of injustice until they turn into a fire in our belly. We need to be able to breathe this fire out of our bodies in some way or we can burn up. Fire is energy. Fire's energy has been harnessed for good or bad by man: heat for survival, lamps lit, industry advanced, cities burned, weapons made, consumption, and more.

If you pass your hand quickly through the flame of a candle, you can withstand it. But prolonged exposure to fire and the human body leaves you with third-degree burns that will scar you past recognition. Look at what fire can do to the skin, a home, and the earth. Understand that the fire of anger and rage can have the same marring impact on physical death. Anger can be a fire of obscurity that will keep you from recognizing your soul's actual ascension. Rage can be a fire that clears the old, dead brush out to usher in the room for the growth of new things.

In the book *Women Who Run with Wolves* by Clarissa Pinkola Estes, Ph. D., she says this about rage: "Even raw and messy emotions can be understood as a form of light, crackling and bursting with energy. We can use the light of rage in a positive way, in order to see into places we cannot normally see. A negative use of rage concentrates destructively in one tiny spot, until like acid creating an ulcer, it burns a black hole right through the delicate layers of the psyche."

Clarissa goes on to say, "But there is another way. All emotion even rage, carries knowledge, insight, what some call enlightenment. Our rage can, for a time, become teacher... a thing not to be rid of so fast, but rather something to climb the mountain for, something to personify via various images in order to learn from, deal with internally, then shape as something useful in the world as a result, or else let it go back down to dust. In a cohesive life, age is not a stand-alone item. It is a substance waiting for our transformative efforts. The cycle of rage is like any other cycle; it rises, falls, dies, and is released as new energy. Attention to the matter of rage begins the process of transformation."

Questions I begin to ask myself and thoughts being formed: What vibrations (hertz) and sound vibrate in the environment by metal weapons clashing together?

There were unmarked bodies on the battlefields of the American Civil War. Vibration off the cannonballs flying through the air caused such bad concussions to soldiers nearby that they would die without being hit.

But there has to be a healthy body component to fighting for what you believe in. Tibetan symbols are metal and chime.

What is the sound of conviction that leads you to fight for what you believe in? What is the sound of righteous anger or sacred rage? What heals the heart when war cries leave the throat, clearing that chakra? What grounding properties are in the intensity of fight? High-intensity workouts, the nervous system, and heart health have to connect in this portion of sacred rage. Inner skeletal muscle promotes the correct functioning of the immune system.

I believe that the Church should begin to learn about the different aspects of strengths amongst the various tribes of Israel. A step further, the Church would benefit from integrating these strengths into the education of all members. I believe that my tribe, the tribe of Benjamin, could teach the other 11 tribes many things about the transmutation of "raw and messy" energy into miracles.

The High Priestess

KARMIC LAW
AND LAW OF GRACE

Everyone wants to put limitations and rules on how your life can map out. I believe there are more rules when dealing with karmic universal laws. Karmic physics governing things like "What you put out will come back tenfold" become obsolete when you are covered by the law of grace.

Christ's Atonement eradicated the need for karma, therefore eliminating the requirement of burnt offerings. Accounts of the veil being torn in the temples are recorded upon Jesus' death. Atonement releasing karma ushers in the release of limitations in this life. When we exercise our priesthood power, we exercise true faith by letting go of the belief of limitation.

Our priesthood power is access to God's power. God is love. By exercising acts of God's love through our faith, the physics of grace can take hold to produce miraculous outcomes.

The veil in a temple when Jesus died was a physical barrier between ordinary life and the temple's sacred space. A torn veil signified defiance of karmic laws that required a man or woman to provide burnt offerings of animal flesh since the time of our first human father, Adam. The term "veil" also takes on an alternative meaning to the one I just described.

The veil is a term used by modern-day Latter-day Saints to signify the separation of the living world and the realm of spirits or God. Piercing or crossing the veil are references to one's ability to contact the other side and commune with Spirit to receive personal revelation. The veil is thinnest in the quiet safety of our temples. The dead come there to receive sacred ordinances from those who still possess a body.

The experience of the physical body's nervous system is a key that unlocks the understanding we need for spiritual progression. Each ordinance is performed with a body present and the binding power of spoken words. The mystery of Heavenly Mother's presence resides in the union of the physical body experience with the piercing of the veil to see our Father's face.

Heavenly Mother's thrones are in the temples. The temples are the safe spaces that Heavenly Father has held for Her through the leadership of the Church of Jesus Christ of Latter-day Saints. The establishment of the Church itself is God's way of creating a home for our Mother and all of their earthly children.

I am no longer bound by the laws of karma because I have committed my life to the law of grace. When I was baptized and endowed with priesthood power in the house of my Father and Mother, I was released from limitations. I surrendered to the overwhelming, reckless love of two omnipotent beings who had a massive plan for me before I inhabited a body.

If I've learned anything about healing trauma through the Atonement of Jesus, it's that it only happens in illogical ways through the Holy Spirit, moving and surrendering the subconscious to be molded by the power of God. Surrender is like jumping into an ocean and not resisting with your muscles or fear, letting the water move your body and going with its current.

On the retreat I mentioned before (led by Keira Poulsen), I decided to overcome a phobia I had acquired during an abusive marriage.

I used to be a great swimmer and diver as a child. I took swim lessons and found comfort in the water. Later in life, while married to a physically, mentally, and sexually abusive man, I developed a phobia of water because he would usually wait until I was in the shower or bath to attack me physically. What once felt like a beautiful communion with nature turned into terror. It hadn't mattered what EMDR therapy I had tried, I could not detach this fear of the water from my body.

Fast forward to the retreat, and there I was, the last person on the dock to jump into a freezing cold lake. My body started shivering, but not from the cold wind outside. The tremors were from my mind and body wrestling with fear. I started crying. With my fellow retreat members and sisters encouraging me onward, I jumped into the water while proclaiming, "I AM DETERMINED!"

Time stopped as though my body was suspended inside the cocoon of water; my body was enveloped. I heard the voice of God say, "YOU are not the fear anymore." I saw the black, ink-like fear in my mind's eye. It ejected from my pores like ink, and then I saw it quickly being pulled away from my body by the water. I emerged from the water a different person. I am not afraid as I was before.

No holds barred anymore. I won't put limitations or expectations on how my purpose will unfold. I haven't been ready before and didn't have exact plans, but I still ran forward, and grace met me where I was. Grace carried me higher than I could have gone alone.

This morning God told me in prayer, "Ask for more."

This is my prayer:

Infinite Spirit, I am asking for more blessings and all that is mine by the birthright of my divine design. I am ready, willing, and able to go where You would lead me. Take me to the Rock that is higher than I am capable of climbing by myself. I know that in my walk with You there is no limit. You, who created me as a sustainer like my Mother, fashioned me as the culminating masterpiece:

woman. *I was yours before I chose my body. I have been yours my whole life. I am yours eternally.*

Thank you for pursuing me constantly.

In and through the light of Christ, I ask for all that is mine, amen.

CONVERSION

There exists a scientific term called "neuroplasticity." Neuroplasticity refers to the brain's ability to form and reorganize synaptic connections in response to learning, experience, or injury. The brain can make new connections and frequent adjustments through cortical remapping.

I have first-hand experience with neuroplasticity through my conversion process. The structure, disciplines, and ordinances of the Church of Jesus Christ of Latter-day Saints assisted me through my efforts of recovery from alcoholism and constant spiritual progression.

Appealing factors for me toward becoming a member of the Church included: 1) The promise of access to unlimited stores of knowledge. I am a lifelong learner and a woman who is constantly thirsty for knowledge. (Learn it all!) 2) Access to work for my ancestors who I could see my whole life. 3) Radical transformation. 4) The ability to access and channel God's power to perform miracles. 5) To be sealed to my mortal family for all time and eternity.

The Church, with its roots in mysticism, has not disappointed me. Through my membership and tenacity of striving, I have gained confidence grounded in my authenticity. Regardless of my external circumstances with toxic church culture, I am grounded in the foundational knowledge that I am a daughter of two heavenly parents who love me for exactly who they made me to be. The woman I am today and the woman I will become has primarily to do with LDS core principles and ordinances. Many of which are unique to the religion.

Conversion is a refining process of transfiguration down to cellular levels when we walk the covenant path and exercise priesthood power. The transmutation of negative energy, thoughts, and epigenetic memory into cleansing, refinement of energy, and opening and refining of energy centers in the body is the miracle of healing. The covenant path affords us a way toward what Deepak Chopra, M.D., defines as "quantum healing" in his book, *Quantum Healing: Exploring the Frontiers of Mind/Body Medicine.*

The term psychosomatic comes to mind. It is defined as, "Caused or aggravated by a mental factor such as internal conflict or stress."

When we make and keep covenants, cellular and genetic cleansing agents provide a spiritual immunity that promotes bodily health. This is why the covenant path has the potential to eradicate generational sin from the genetic code so that it doesn't pass on to children. You cannot eliminate all generational sin without females also exercising priesthood power. Conversion doesn't exist without successful change via neuroplasticity in the form of consistent behaviors in line with exercising priesthood power.

A mind/body interconnectedness is required to actualize all concepts, doctrine, and covenants of the Church of Jesus Christ of Latter-day Saints. Abilities are not entitled to only one gender.

Both divine female and male energy are required from the alignment of a human body to form a Merkaba so that the human soul can commune with revelation from God. You cannot have the results you want if you do not understand and implement the importance of both Heavenly Father AND Heavenly Mother.

We don't know much about Heavenly Mother because the Bible was not translated to its correct meaning. If you want to know more about our Mother, our origins, and Heavenly Mother's essence, we must go back to the seed of word meanings.

God is the word and the word was God. With the intent of His heart to speak the world into existence, God formed this world for us. Let's go to the etymology of our Abrahamic religion to find answers.

CONVERSION AS A CHURCH: A WOLF IN THE LION'S DEN
Vision on March 25, 2022 at Keira Poulsen's retreat

I saw the City of Enoch hovering above the desert ground. A circle of twelve women hovered above the city. Chords of light came from each of the women's bodies upward to tie together. The chords all created an enormous star in the shape of a Merkaba.

I then saw myself in the form of my "highest self" or myself without the limitations of a physical body. I was a giantess, strong like a horse with gigantic wings. I was trying to go into the mouth of a tunnel under a temple that looked like a marble cave. Carved above the entrance read: "The Lion's Den." I was unable to fit into the opening with my current heavenly body, so I had to become something smaller. I watched myself morph into a wolf. I was able to enter the "Lion's Den" as a wolf and I charged into the underbelly of the temple.

I then saw all of the temples uprooting all over the world. They all had roots to them, like plants that were uprooted to go into a new environment to grow. It reminded me of the seedlings in a greenhouse that get replanted on the grounds of the temple when it's their turn to reach maturity. All of the temples that were uprooted gravitated to the temple I had gone into. They all sped up when they got closer to the temple that I was in and began colliding into the temple. But they were not colliding to be destroyed. They were on a collision course of revision and began to fit together like Tetris cubes. As the temples formed together in harmonious ways, they settled to become an entire white city.

Once the new structure settled into the ground, roots began to grow that ran so deep that they derived sustenance from the earth's very core.

God told me that this vision is what is possible for the restoration of brokenness in the Church of Jesus Christ of Latter-day Saints if I choose to go forward as a member of the tribe of Benjamin to enact change.

CONVERSION OF MYSELF
March 28, 2022

I am a shadow worker. What happened to me was a jailbreak conversion.

I am locked inside a high tower of the adversary. I sit, watching the light of the Father pouring through the jail cell window. The arched pattern of light falls to the ground, my only marker of a day going by. I watch it slowly creep toward my naked toes—feet flat on the cold, stone ground.

Something about today is different. As I look at the beams from the window, I can decipher some pattern inside the light. It doesn't quite look like numbers or symbols. Maybe an alien language I know nothing about? I watch the gradient of piercing bright light slope toward my body in various degrees of intensity until I reach myself. I am engulfed in the absence of light.

I understand that I am not fully darkness. I know there is light and shadow and degrees of darkness in me.

The stone cell is all that I know with various beings, not of my kind, coming in and out of the cell throughout my life. They bring their alien weapons and test them on me. I am afraid, but I don't know what to do to make it stop. I do not know if there is any other way besides surrendering to the pain until they stop. No one has equipped me with a weapon of my own. I don't know what fighting back even means.

On days like today, when the light is strong and brilliant, the shadow beings do not enter my cell. They have a resistance to the language of the light I am now seeing in playful, searing tones. The light language dances like an invitation. I have learned patience by this point in my life. I am not patient by nature, but by discipline. I slowly reach toward the light with my heavy shackles.

Lifting these heavy restraints on a daily basis has allowed my body and mind to grow stronger. As my wrist reaches the dancing language, it organizes like a page of language on the metal. It asks a question to my energy. It is not out loud and I allow my heart to say, "Yes." The shackles cannot withstand the dancing. The metal is made of contractual agreements with the shadow beings who inflict confusion in my mind. I watch the light as it dances over my skin. Instead of breaking me, the light seeps in.

A deafening shaking starts rocking my cell. The bondage breaks and the wall splits from the top through to the earth.

I am falling. I think I might die. The cell is the only world I have ever known.

To my surprise, I do not die. I land softly and my heart hears, "Go to the armory."

I don't know what this means, but I run back toward the stone castle I just fell from. I push through the rubble and I see a door. The door is as high as the tower was and I PUSH it. The door is surprisingly light.

As I cross the threshold of the door, I look down to see my skin clean. My forearms and chest are covered by soft armor. My body feels safe in this new covering and I stand up as tall as I can. I feel a new sensation of pride and honor. I feel ordained to do some work with my body.

Another message comes through. This time the communication is cool and free-flowing. I feel as though I am drinking cool water. There is a thirst that is quenched within me as I receive a message from this voice.

"Look around. You know the purpose of these weapons and you must teach others what they are used for. You must teach the way against these weapons."

My eyes reach upwards and away from my new body discovery. I am not afraid even though I do not fully understand. I do not know the limitations of my body simply because I am what might be labeled "different" or "bad."

I only know what I am capable of.

I want to use my capabilities to free others trapped in tall towers like I once was. I want to be what I am naturally.

I reach up and pull down a weapon from the wooden racks on a stone wall. I feel the cold, but I am still warmth.

I am not afraid of this weapon even though my whole life it has been used against me, against my mind, and against my body by entities who have no names.

I carry this weapon out and away, not to use it for harm, but to dismantle it.

To understand and to teach light warfare.

To teach others how to come out of the darkness into various depths of light (known as shadows) until the light of the sun can be withstood. There is still darkness in me, but it is not arranged differently now that I am no longer just looking at shadows on the wall.

The women are a soul vehicle to not just bring their family earthside as babies but to heal their family's past, present, and future. The family is the seed of the full restoration of Christ's church on earth. Harmony on a cultural level makes possible the modern-day rapture of unified vibration to elevate the Church toward its potential of spiritual progression to touch the face of God. If the human body can aid in spiritual progression when in alignment, then the body or members of the Church require harmony in working together to experience Joseph Smith's vision for this Church.

What I am really talking about with this book is the restorative power that the Atonement has on what was broken. The blended family is a form of restoration. The healing of the cultural toxicity and generational trauma is a form of restoration.

This is the restored church of Christ. It is critical that we acknowledge the places in the Church that are currently still breeding shame. Using the salve of the Atonement and the universal laws of grace, we are able to take pain and refine it to remove imperfections and create elements and weapons fashioned as the full armor of God to protect our families.

In this way, Jesus has taken on another form of workmanship as a spiritual blacksmith. We always have the choice to alchemize the energies of pain through Christ's Atonement toward full body/mind/spirit healing in the refiner's fire.

Conversion as a whole LDS population is vital to receive abundance and elevate (like with anti-gravity) the Church to the level of the City of Enoch. The universe will always send us experiences and lessons that match the energetic frequency of the vibrations that we are putting out from our bodies. We receive the same cycles if we don't change our mindsets or behavior until we learn and shift.

My grandmother told me that if we don't learn our lessons, God will continue to send us the same hardships or experiences until we

DO know. Then we are free to discover the next lesson. She was talking about the physics of the law of vibration.

In his online article entitled "What is the Law of Vibration," Mataeo Smith says, "The main point of this law is that we all have a specific vibrational frequency, and that you may learn to modify your vibration if you're in a low vibrational situation or experience. According to the law, the more attuned you are to your own energy, the more you will notice how your vibrations influence your entire experience.

"Theorists say by choosing and directing our ideas, we have the ability to control the frequency of our being. The vibration of your body is determined by your emotional moods. And, to a considerable part, these vibrations determine how you live your life because they create resonance with anything that vibrates at the same frequency."

THE HIGH PRIESTESS

I am more wolf than woman.
I am a ravenous high priestess.
I am a Benjamite convert.
I am a sentinel of mother.
I'm a hunter.
Treat me like fire burning,
because I'm not stopping.
"I'm going hunting."

"Benjamin is a ravenous wolf; in the morning
he shall devour the prey, and at night he shall divide the spoil."
-Genesis 49:27

The blessing of Benjamin comes in two parts. In Genesis 49, the patriarch, Jacob, gathers his sons when he feels his death is near. The sons gathered to him and he gave each of his sons a blessing. Each of Jacob's sons became a progenitor of one of the twelve tribes of Israel. The quote above (from Genesis 49:27) is the blessing given to Benjamin by Jacob.

The tribe of Benjamin has an innate war-like nature, and that's why I believe the ravenous wolf was depicted in the blessing. The blessing being in two parts spoke to me as a past/future and for better/for worse dynamic based on the agency we have to choose which side of the coin a Benjamite aligns with. There is an inherent blood lust and warrior ethos of my kind. I have learned to temper this to forge myself into a weapon of light for my Heavenly Parents. The duality and dichotomy of carnal man vs. enlightened being is a complicated task that members of the tribe of Benjamin must iron out.

There was a point during the writing of this book when I hit a major "faith crisis" and was angry at God. I raged and demanded that He tell me why He would push me toward aligning with a Church that had such intense inclusion issues because my experience has been that I have become lonelier in this journey. I have lost friends for my decision to convert to this religion, had attacks toward my family unit, and had aspects ripped from me. In defiance, I stated that I would no longer listen to anyone in the Church who wasn't a Benjamite because I needed to know the truth from my own tribe.

Over the next three days, I had three people contact me who had been following my conversion journey over social media. They had understood my posts in the way that I speak and my journey through recovering from alcoholism and they wanted to follow the same path forward into enlightenment. They asked me to lead them toward resources to overcome addiction and then asked me about talking to missionaries.

This was a clear answer from my Father, who I warred with three days prior. I said out loud, "Oh. My tribe still needs to come into the Church and I have a role in gathering them to this place."

Then God dropped in with His stern tone, "There is much more work to be done by you. Push it out."

I am a stubborn child, but I am obedient to the will of my Father. Eventually. So, here I am. Doing. The. Work.

PATRIARCHAL BLESSINGS IN THE CHURCH TODAY

The tradition of receiving a blessing in the Church has continued into the current practices of Latter-day Saints. Each stake, marked by geographical boundaries, has a patriarch assigned to it. The patriarch's role is to receive revelation for each member's life. The revelations are written down for the member to refer to throughout their life. Usually, the patriarchal blessing is accepted in the years of adolescence, but it can be when a member of the Church decides that it is time for them to receive it. Sadly, even some members who have been a part of the Church for years have not yet received their patriarchal blessing. If you are reading this and are a member who has not yet done this for yourself, go do it. You will be blessed beyond measure. The blessings serve as a compass when navigating the ocean of this realm of existence. I would like to add that my patriarchal blessing has allowed me to see myself as my Heavenly Parents see me.

I made an appointment with my bishop to discuss scheduling my patriarchal blessing. I was sitting outside of the bishop's office and a member of my ward (who is now deceased), Dennis Johnson, was also waiting in the chairs. His daughter talked to the bishop about early morning seminary classes for high school.

Dennis was a very present man and could easily pick up on the emotional climate of other people. One of his best qualities was that he had no fear of telling people exactly how he felt at the moment. It is a trait that I admired about him. His obedience to act on the promptings he received from the Holy Spirit made him an incredible disciple of the Savior.

I was grateful that his daughter's meeting with the bishop was running behind that day because what Dennis told me was priceless. We talked about my desire to receive my patriarchal blessing. He said that he was proud of my willingness to step into that space of asking to receive blessings. He said, "The Lord always wants to bless us, but He often waits for us to JUST ask."

This seed Dennis planted into my mind would eventually grow into a flourishing daily prayer: "Father, I am grateful for all you have given me. More, please. I am ready to receive all that You have in store for my life."

Our Heavenly Parents are in the realm of infinite possibility, the highest ideals of our hearts, and constantly in the energy of creating abundance. They have designed us to reach these great heights too.

What would happen for you if you let it be easy and just asked for blessings in your own life?

The day that I was to receive my patriarchal blessing, the stake patriarch gave a talk in our ward sacrament meeting. I could feel a familiar soul language emanating from his speech. One of the aspects of this patriarch that I felt was meant for me specifically was that he cannot see. I felt that this was the patriarch for me because I have felt judged based on my stature and appearance my entire adult life. There would have been an element of skepticism about the blessing I received if the patriarch had been able to see my physical appearance.

About an hour after our church meeting, I went to receive my patriarchal blessing with my husband. My husband and I have had a distinctive experience of him being present for or performing all of the ordinances on my full conversion and spiritual progression. I cannot talk too much about what was received, but BOTH of my Heavenly Parents kept chiming in during that experience to give revelation on the purpose of my life.

During the patriarchal blessing, I was assigned to the tribe of Benjamin. I went digging in scripture about Benjamites. I am a deep thinker and I thought, "If I am of Benjamin then there must be more that I can learn from others in the Bible who are also from this tribe."

BENJAMITES IN THE BIBLE

There aren't many of us in the Bible, let's just start there. The ones who are mentioned in scripture are impactful, whether that be for better or worse. They're either evil to the max and burning cities to the ground or delivering entire races of people from wickedness.

The members of the tribe in the Bible include the first King of Israel, Saul, the apostle Paul, the left-handed warrior Ehud, Mordecai, and Esther.

I know that Benjamin is the smallest tribe of the twelve, but I also believe that the blessing of the tribe being divided means that there are still many more that will step forward and heed a call in the end times when their warrior ethos is needed most. As far as I know, right now the Church is mainly from the tribe of Ephriam.

I believe that this impacts the Church culture because each tribe has a distinct soul language and method of receiving revelation. I also think that unless members of the tribe of Benjamin step into the space of the Church and learn to translate, then Benjamites outside of the Church will not hear the wolf call or understand the importance of integrating into the Church. Benjamites are needed as the war increases in intensity. Learning the endurance, strategy, and knowledge of my tribe is a necessary component of combating the adversary.

TRIBAL MENTALITY

I also believe that church culture would vastly improve with the study and integration of tribal mentality. Nomadic and tribal cultures of ancient to present times held healthier spaces of reverence for cultivating respect around female power and Heavenly Mother.

HIGH PRIESTESSES & INITIATORY

Before the endowment ordinance takes place, an individual goes through the ordinance of the initiatory. From my understanding, female priesthood holders are the members assigned to perform this initiatory, which is a blessing over the body to prepare the body for receiving priesthood power.

The priesthood power of a woman is utilized for the purpose of blessing the physical body and that fact is not a coincidence. This is an indicator of exercising female priesthood power everywhere.

ENHEDUANNA

Enheduanna (ca. 2334–2279 BC) was the EN high priestess of the moon goddess in ancient Mesopotamia. Her father, King Sargon, gave her the position of high priestess. To be the high priest or priestess was the highest religious, political, and economic appointment of that time, second to the king.

Enheduanna wrote a collection of hymns that ended up uniting her father's entire kingdom. Regardless of her religious beliefs, the results of her position show the power that women have to connect populations toward a harmonic output. At the time, her country served different gods, yet she was able to bring them together. This is also a testament to the power of music (resonance and hertz) and words (sound put to intention).

The most remarkable thing about her was that she is the first recorded author to identify herself in her writing.

A PAGAN AND A CHRISTIAN
WALK INTO A BAR:
PAGANISM & CHRISTIANITY

"We claim the privilege of worshiping Almighty God according to the dictates of our own conscience, and allow all men the same privilege, let them worship how, where, or what they may."
-The eleventh Article of Faith,
written in 1842 by the Prophet Joseph Smith. (The Articles of Faith are 13 statements that explain the basic doctrines and practices of The Church of Jesus Christ of Latter-day Saints.)

Religion and politics have always engaged in incestuous relationships throughout world history. If a Pagan and a Christian walk into the same space, you will likely see a holy war. The wars were not about bringing religion to another part of the world. If you take the time to learn about the varying aspects of any given war, you'll see that it's almost always about acquiring more land or resources. The current ruler wishes to amass wealth and declare a more significant imprint of personal legacy in world history.

Wars result in bloodshed and the eradication of whole earthbound cultures. I am primarily Celtic, so the cultures that inhabited the regions my ancestors are from were Picts, Druidic spirituality, and Norse polytheistic paganism. The ancient Celtic people were not interested in forcing dominion over new territories.

Ancient Celts were very spiritual and received spiritual guidance from Druids. Druids taught spiritual enlightenment and knowledge orally so that the practices would stay close to the people.

Cross-pollination of Pagan and Christian traditions is present now in the timing and ways we celebrate holidays. The assimilation of Pagan holidays, such as Ostara becoming Easter, Samhain becoming Halloween, etc., was a compromise to appease forced conversions of Pagans to Christianity.

Now we keep this tradition of silenced voices within the culture of our religious practices while not wanting to mention any belief system outside of our own. If we are willing to assimilate, we must be glad to be more open-minded about integration and inclusion on all levels.

I was once approached about my openness to talk about the pagan religions of my ancestors. I mentioned how the sacrament is a reenactment of cannibalism as we practice a weekly ritual of eating the flesh and drinking the blood of a man who gave His life for our sins.

It is absurd that we are not acknowledging the integration of the Pagan-based ritualistic idealism that enables us to access powers of renewal. If we talk about it, it is labeled as "bad" or "wrong." Some will have their temple recommendations rebuked regardless of their high fidelity to covenant-keeping because they have open minds.

The seer stone used by the prophet Joseph Smith is an ancient Celtic practice of seership. Celtic people by origin are pagans. It is a natural assumption of mine to conclude that Joseph probably had some Celtic genetic memory of translating through a seer stone to have had this capability naturally.

I understand that the ordinances that we perform in the Church are a form of ritual that allows us a renewal of spirit and refinement on the path toward seeing our Heavenly Parents again. In the denial and condemnation of "OTHER," we are rebuking the Holy Spirit from giving us the understanding we need to worship to the dictates of what our personal soul needs to see and hear God.

The book *Wise Women*, edited by Susan Cahill, states, "Theologian Elizabeth Johnson's description of God in *She Who Is* as 'relational aliveness,' as masculine/feminine force of mutuality, implies open-heartedness and change as signs of the presence of a holy spirit."

Here is the mind-blowing revelation I received while writing this book. Pagans and Christian-based religions may not be so different after all. It is my belief that earthbound religions have more insight into the manifestations of power of our Heavenly Mother. I believe that they have a better understanding of Heavenly Mother than the patriarchal religious structures seen in Christianity and Abrahamic religions.

Abrahamic religions and pagan religions are two depictions of equal yet different God or Source energies—divine masculine and divine feminine energies. Neither is complete without acknowledging the truth of the other. They are two separate belief systems trying to arrive at the same destination of enlightenment.

We cannot ignore that patriarchal religions have dominated and subdued female voices in the plan of happiness. The male members of the Church need to listen and learn from female perspectives. In his General Conference address in April of 2022, Ronald A. Rasband stated, "I remembered who I was and I stood to bare my witness." Women also have the birthright to stand and witness miracles performed by our application of priesthood power. A study of cultures that treated women with high regard, specifically nomadic cultures like the Scythian nomads, should be used to break old narratives.

Men are tied to the women for all time and eternity through the ordinance of sealing families together. It is an act of self-love to allow free expression and integration of divine female revelation into the narrative and progression of the Church.

Women are able to worship according to their intuition. Men need to hold safe space for women exercising their priesthood power. Women unapologetically sharing what they receive and how they worship are women exercising their priesthood power.

Quotes from the book *Wise Women*, edited By Susan Cahill, that I wanted to share:

- "The light of wisdom—the truth of things—that radiate from the actual, often dense circumstances of life have inspired many writing women to transform their understanding and intuitions into language."
- "Wise love, generous action, practical vision, a belief in the reality of the invisible are the core truths of many of the narratives represented."
- "Perhaps because it has been women's task throughout history 'to go on believing in life when there was almost no hope,' in the words of Margaret Mead, women have sought and cultivated the goods of the spirit out of a practical need for meaning. The varieties of significance they have intuited amid vast fields of lived experience have illumined their understanding and shaped the strategies of the journey, making the hard going sometimes easier, sometimes blessed, more promising than opaque. And meaning, the traveler's sustaining wisdom, is its own reward. A destination in the country of solidarities."
- "Women have always found the world of the spirit compelling for a number of reasons. One is their historical exclusion from the full exercise of their spiritual identities within religious institutions; that injustice raises consciousness is cliche by now, however it is true."

"OCCULT" OR
UNEDUCATED?

A ridiculous infiltration of the "occult" mindset is taking hold in the culture of the Church. One day, I met with a woman for lunch who was going through an intense life challenge and she needed support. She was intrigued by my conversion and asked a lot of questions about my journey.

As we were talking, she told me that she had recently had her temple recommendation revoked because she had crystals and gemstones in her home. I was greatly disturbed by this and asked if she had taken this issue up any higher than her bishop. She said that she had, but that the stake president agreed with the bishop of her ward. She felt lost and had been a devout member of the Church of Jesus-Christ of Latter-day Saints. Her experience with leadership made her want to leave the Church altogether.

THE BREASTPLATE OF AARON

Moses' brother, Aaron, was three years older than Moses. Aaron was the first high priest appointed during the time of Moses. Aaron wore a breastplate over his robe. On the breastplate were 12 gemstones that represented the 12 tribes of Israel. The stones were believed to have metaphysical properties that functioned to help the vital organs of the body function properly.

These stones were also believed to aid the person wearing them to more easily receive revelation from God. In Exodus 28, Moses sets out specific instructions for how Aaron's garments should be made.

In Revelations 21, there is also a list of 12 stones. Other references for this breastplate can be found in the 1 Thessalonians 5:8 (KJV), Revelations 9:9 (KJV), Doctrine and Covenants 17:1, and Joseph Smith—History 1:35, 42, and 52.

BROTHER OF JARED

In the Book of Mormon, the book of Ether Chapters tells us how the Brother of Jared ventured to the top of a mountain with 16 stones to ask God to touch them so that he could light the barges. It was through the Brother of Jared's faith that God showed Himself to the Brother of Jared and lit the stones.

NOAH'S ARC

At several points in the voyage of Noah and his arc, it was so dark at night that only the light of a gemstone (what is believed to be garnet) illuminated the unending sea. The gemstone is referenced several times in the Bible.

JOSEPH SMITH AND THE SEER STONE

The most infamous story of stones in the LDS religion is Joseph Smith translating the Book of Mormon through the use of a stone. "Seer stones" were a type of divination tool that dates back to ancient Celtic practices of seership.

I am now curious about Joseph Smith's genetic lineage if he was able to have this ability without any practice or instruction. The genetic predisposition of certain gifts exists because of epigenetics. Scientists are now finding that memories of our ancestors can be passed through DNA, much like phobias.

These are just a few examples of stones being utilized for healing and containers of light in the scriptures. It is a worldly patriarchal construct to label the use of crystals, gemstones, or sedimentary rock as "occult." Furthermore, it is a construct of unrighteous dominion and toxic church culture to condemn those who naturally understand these conduits for healing and personal revelation.

There is a fundamental reason that stones have been used for centuries as adornments for the human body in the form of jewelry and it wasn't just to "look pretty." Holding certain stones (all stones having different vibrations based on where in the earth they were formed) elicits a reaction from the body while also promoting the health of the body.

The High Priestess

HISTORY OF
WESTERN WOMEN

The history of women in Western ideology and culture profoundly impacts how women behave within the patriarchal society in the United States today. We have been taught to dig a grave for the sources of our strength. Females going through puberty don't lack aggressive impulses compared to their male counterparts. A fork in the road exists in adolescence for females to dull down physical violence and turn toward methods of injurious behavior. Instead, women learn means of psychological warfare or what researchers call "indirect aggression."

According to Finnish psychologist Kaj Björkqvist, indirect aggression is "a kind of social manipulation." He says, "The aggressor manipulates others to attack the victim, or, by other means, makes use of the social structure in order to harm the target person, without being personally involved in the attack. (...) The more able the aggressor is at staying out of reach of the opponent, and at assessing the opponent's retaliation resources, the better [she] will be at avoiding counter-attack and minimizing risks."

Indirect aggression becomes more appealing than packing a punch to adolescent girls because of the way Western culture has told stories about violent women. Violent women or women outside of cultural "norms" have always been construed as witches, whores, and pariahs. An example is the U.S. history of prostitution in the early West. Madams of brothels and prostitutes were pioneering female entrepreneurship in a time when only men were allowed to control money and own property in the United States.

Before any suffragette movements eventually gave women the right to vote, we had the tough, ambitious madams of parlor houses and brothels taking the West by the reins. These women were just as wild as the males who had ventured to the Wild West, seeking money and adventure. Maybe even more so as the average frontier ratio was two women to every 100 men in 1849 (Seagraves).

Death, abuse, and poor living conditions were among the brutalities of daily life. Of course, many horrors of the professional occupation plagued prostitutes in red-light districts. But we cannot sidestep the contributions some of these women made to the communities in which they lived. Doing so would be a blatant disservice to their lives on this earth.

Excerpt from *Soiled Doves: Prostitution in the Early West* by Ann Seagraves:

"Although the madams were among the early entrepreneurs, historians often fail to recognize their significant contributions to the Western economy. These enterprising women, who played an important role within their communities, were never invited to join or attend a commercial club. They were not accepted by society, and, in most cases, denied the protection of the law, due to their profession.

"Collectively, their businesses employed the largest group of women on the frontier. They supplied a home for thousands of females who would have otherwise been forced to live on the streets.

"The majority of madams owned their own real estate, and all provided a considerable amount of revenue to their city or town. They paid property, school and county taxes, license fees and filled the pockets of corrupt officials and police officers. The society that did not respect these businesswomen, nonetheless, expected them to donate generously to churches and local charities. Merchants, who profited off of the ladies, overcharged them for liquor, food and personal goods. In order to run a successful business, with a substantial return, the western madam had to have a great deal of patience and more than the usual amount of business acumen."

One madam and the working girls of her brothel nursed an entire community back to health when smallpox hit the town and nobody else would care for the men. Regardless of the amount of service, donations, and taxes paid by madams, they were not allowed to be buried within the gates of town cemeteries. Neither were the women who chose prostitution as a profession. Prostitutes of the early Western frontier faced even more extreme prejudice once the refined women arrived in town with their husbands. A former prostitute of the early West found herself the victim of a fatal, mysterious poisoning once she left her former employment and married. The person who had poisoned her was never discovered. The woman had endured countless hardships from the women in her community before her death. For what? Wanting an everyday life?

A similar dynamic exists in the culture of the female members of the Church accepting new converts. Female outliers, pariahs, mavericks, and Benjamites need to be able to take up space. Contributions of outlier women could only benefit Church operations.

As I read through Anne Seagraves' book, I noted another dynamic regarding tithing and Church structure that should be addressed.

I am currently in my mid-thirties. I have developed an enormous resistance to paying my tithing as I have elevated in the ranks of income-earning while listening to the narrative of Heavenly Mother get shut down again and again. My husband has to pay it for me because I struggle so much with it.

This struggle of loving the Church and knowing things have to change is prevalent in female members of modern-day Zion. Many leave silently and deal with a faith transition that compounds their already present grief of unsaid words about their experiences.

I empathize with lifelong female members who are barely hanging on as members of the Church. I have hit at least 20 different "faith crises" writing this book. I have entertained throwing my hands in the air and leaving the Church. God won't let me. He drops in that I have to talk about it and not just go silently. So, here I am, hoping that my voice will ring the bell to give notice to pertinent issues that can be radically improved with the proper adjustments. Advocacy, feminism, and intellect of pioneer women in the Church have been a catalyst for policy and procedural change in the past. I am hoping to add my name to that list of women.

Like the madams mentioned above, whose community leadership expected massive donations while still treating them like pariahs, I do not WANT to donate my money to an organization with leadership that discourages me from actualizing my priesthood power.

Fear mongering and shaming will not silence me on these topics. Exercising my voice unapologetically is an exercise of my priesthood power. Burning out of old stagnancy to usher in new growth is a specific component of female priesthood power. Cycling out old to bring in new life is what my body does monthly.

If anything in my book offends you, I invite you to be offended about the underlying factors that have manifested these real-life experiences as a new convert to this Church and help me change them. In this reactive defense of your brain to information that contradicts your already formed beliefs, I would like to invite you to separate yourself from your ego and realize this reaction is an indication that we are really on the same page.

I am a champion for the Church to operate to its highest efficiency, so I keep writing. Regardless of anything I bring up in this book or my feelings about it all, I know that this is the straightest path I've found to transfiguration from carnal to enlightened.

I am running from my core personality traits writing this book in the way my brain can disassemble how things are not working to figure out how to put them back together so they function better. I am championing for the women who have left, the women barely hanging on, and the women who will be new converts.

WE NEED WOMEN NOW

If you are a woman I have mentioned, I am petitioning you to keep holding the line with me. Don't be silent; advocate for yourself and others like you. If you have stories of inappropriate conduct of leadership presiding over your wards, stakes, etc., go higher within the chain of command in the Church until change can be made. What happened to you is not your fault. Don't believe the lies from the adversary that keep you silent. We have to hold the line on these issues and cannot assume that higher-ups in the Church know what the problems are. We have to voice them.

GENERATIONAL SHIFTS

Those of us raising children in today's world are drowning—trying to navigate LDS blended family parenting under the old-fashioned, standard nuclear family way. It's not working for all of us, so we are naturally adapting to our environmental stressors for the optimal survival of our families.

FEMALE ENTREPRENEURSHIP AND TITHING

A significant gender role shift is that women my age earn higher incomes. Brands that provide products and services are marketing to my age group because the women and wealth statistics are rising with us. This creates a shift in the home life toward men staying at home while the wife brings home the bacon. The need for a parent at home with children is definitely pressing, with the trailblazing female spouse, who has the highest income-earning potential, out in the world. If you can make money as a woman, why wouldn't you? If your spouse or significant other can make more money than you, why wouldn't you encourage her to do that?

High income earning automatically raises a woman's standards, and therefore, her vibrational output becomes faster like the current of a river. If the money of women (interchange the word money with energy) is expected, but the contribution of our wisdom and intuition is rebuked, the loss of numbers (membership, tithing, marriages) will be significantly increased.

As time progresses, the inclusion of women and priesthood power roles within the Church will only become more critical to maintaining church attendance, participation in callings, statistics of full-tithe payers, and families maintaining membership in the Church. I have had women disclose that they would even be willing to come back into the Church if there was more freedom to talk about Heavenly Mother and more of a place for women acting in their priesthood power. Therein lies an aspect of "gathering scattered Israel" that is perhaps not often thought of.

WE NEEDED WOMEN
THEN PIONEER WOMEN

"Be kind to the women. They constitute half of the
population and are mothers to the other half. (...) My dear
sisters, you marvelous women ... I stand in great admiration
for all you do. I see your hands in everything."
- President Gordon B. Hinckley,
2003 General Conference address

Pioneer women of the Church of Jesus Christ of Latter-day Saints
were a cornerstone of so many aspects of the Church and,
unfortunately, I cannot name them all in this section. I will highlight
some of the incredible women from my lineage and women who
significantly contributed to foundational aspects of our current
establishment financially and with policy in the early years of the
Church.

The Word of Wisdom, female missionary work, female
advancement initiatives, and service in the form of Relief Society
all came from female members of the Church.

Here are some intelligent, go-getting women from early Church
history that you may not have heard of.

EMILY SOPHIA TANNER RICHARDS (1850-1929)

After reading her life story, I have a deep admiration for Emily
Sophia Tanner Richards. I feel like we are kindred spirits.

Emily Tanner married Franklin Snyder Richards in 1869. Franklin Richards worked as legal counsel for the LDS Church, but her marriage is not what makes her spectacular to me.

Emily was a perfect example of the balance of divine masculine and feminine energy that we can achieve while reaching our full stature here on earth. She was able to balance life as a mother, wife, and member of the Church. She was actively involved (with the endorsement of the First Presidency) with the women's suffragette movement and even personally knew Susan B. Anthony.

An online article on Deseret News explains, "In addition to serving for more than 30 years on the Relief Society General Board, Emily Richards proposed that Utah organize a suffrage group affiliated with the National Woman Suffrage Association. She formed friendships with such leaders as Susan B. Anthony, Anna Howard Shaw, and Carrie Chapman Catt" (Toone).

According to a profile written by Radke-Moss in *Women of Faith in the Latter Days, Vol. 3*, "Her beliefs in change and charity fed into a vast movement of activism for peace and social justice, and she believed strongly in the restored gospel while also promoting progressive political views ... Richards was well-traveled and well-spoken, the model wife, mother, friend, hostess and individual ... a Relief Society and YLMIA leader ... and advocate for the helpless."

MARTHA MARIA HUGHES CANNON (1857-1932)

I am sure that Martha had the most exciting dinner table conversation because in 1896, as a Democrat, she defeated her own Republican husband in a political race to become the first female senator in United States History.

An excerpt from a Deseret News online article states: "'Mattie,' as she was called, was also a physician, trained lecturer, women's rights advocate and suffragist, a wife, mother and a member of The Church of Jesus Christ of Latter-day Saints."

As a teenager, Cannon worked as a typesetter for the Deseret News and worked for the *Woman's Exponent*, a women's newspaper. In time, she enrolled at the University of Michigan School of Medicine and graduated in 1881. Then she moved to Philadelphia to attend the University of Pennsylvania Auxiliary School of Medicine and was the only woman in her class. She graduated in 1882 with a degree in pharmacy. She also attended the National School of Elocution and Oratory in Philadelphia.

She returned to Utah and married Angus M. Cannon to become the fourth of his six plural wives. She had three children with him.

Cannon took an interest in local politics and women's suffrage, which led her to run as one of five Democrats for state senator. As mentioned, she won, and she served two terms in the legislature with a specific interest in issues related to public health.

After leaving politics, she served as a member of the Utah Board of Health and as a member of the board for the Utah State School for the Deaf and Dumb.

After her husband's death in 1915, she settled in California and continued to practice medicine. She died in Los Angeles in 1932.

"'Beyond her legacy as the first woman to hold the office of state senator … she must also be remembered as an activist for the cause of women, a mother, a physician and a devoted Latter-day Saint,' wrote Stapley and Lieber" (Turley and Nash).

ELIZABETH ANN CLARIDGE MCCUNE (1852-1924)

Another excerpt from the Deseret News article shares this about Elizabeth Ann Claridge McCune: "In 1898, Joseph McMurrin of the European mission presidency wrote to the First Presidency that 'if a number of bright and intelligent women were called on missions to England, the results would be excellent.'"

As a result, the First Presidency decided to call and set apart single sister missionaries.

Elizabeth Ann Claridge McCune was instrumental in McMurrin's decision to write the letter. Raised in Utah and Nevada, McCune married her childhood sweetheart, a successful businessman named Alfred W. McCune.

In 1897, the McCunes embarked on a tour of Europe. While sightseeing, Elizabeth also planned to do some genealogical research. In preparation, she requested a priesthood blessing from LDS Church President Lorenzo Snow. During the blessing, he said, "Thy mind shall be as clear as an angel's when explaining the principles of the gospel."

While in Europe, Elizabeth McCune accompanied the full-time missionaries to street meetings. She wanted to share the gospel like the elders.

After a former member of the Church spread an anti-Mormon message in the community, McMurrin called on McCune to speak to a large crowd. Although nervous, her words helped to dispel the false message, and it became evident that women could reach hearts in a way the elders could not.

"This incident opened my eyes as to the great work our sisters could do," she wrote of the experience.

As a result of McCune's experience, Amanda Inez Knight and Lucy Jane Brimhall were set apart as the first single female proselytizing missionaries in LDS Church history on April 1, 1898. They were both assigned to the European Mission.

JENNETTE SNEDDEN DUNCAN (APRIL 21, 1830 - JULY 28, 1914)

Jennette was my 5th great-grandmother who left behind a sizable inheritance and a sweetheart in Gartsherrie, Lanarkshire, Scotland to venture to America. She was on the same ship as her future husband, James Duncan, a Scotsman. They remained acquainted after landing in Pennsylvania and got married before traveling to Utah. James Duncan worked for Anson Call during that part of their life.

In 1857, James and Jennette relocated to settle in Meadow, Utah. Living conditions were not excellent, and they took refuge near a ridge. True to her Scottish origins, Jennette was a stubborn and determined woman. Her fortitude served her family and religion well. She was known to consistently walk a long distance to "attend to her religious duties" as her great-granddaughter wrote in her life sketch. There was an instance when she was walking a long distance in the snow and almost froze to death. A carriage passing by refused to give her a ride. Before it had a chance to pass her completely, she grabbed the back of it and held on for a ride anyways. She became so cold she eventually fell off and the woman inside the carriage made her husband pick my great (x5) grandmother up and let her in.

Jennette was a skilled seamstress. She made clothing and hats for her newly budding LDS community. Her great-granddaughter, LaVeda Duncan wrote, "She worked very hard all of her life both in the home, garden, and in the fields. She was always good and kind to her family and did all she could to make them happy. The neighbor's children liked to come to her house because she always fed them when they were hungry. Her whole married life was a very hard one, but she remained faithful and was loved by all who knew her."

This woman would never return to her Scottish homeland before she died. She was willing to leave everything she knew behind to devote her life and talents to establishing the Church of Jesus Christ of Latter-day Saints.

Women came from all over the country and globe to pioneer this Church. Along with Jennette and James Duncan as Early Pioneers, I have several notable women of early LDS history in my lineage. Several women in my family were set apart for callings of midwifery by early church prophets. These women safely delivered hundreds and hundreds of babies earthside.

It has been a blessing to read their stories and see the resemblance of strength that I share with them because they are a part of who I am.

ADAM AND EVE &
THE ABRAHAMIC SEED

The LDS religion focuses heavily on the first man, Adam, and our first mother, Eve. I grew up attending different denominational Christian churches. Whenever Eve was brought up, shame was attached to her decision to eat the apple in the garden of Eden. Eve eating the apple was a "wrong choice," for which I would atone with my bodily pain through childbirth, menstruation, and my submissiveness to men. Women were not equal to men in this narrative. We were a form of subman—a consolation prize.

I carried within me a deeply instilled shame of being female and acted on that shame through the decisions in my life. How can you value your life as sacred if you are taught that God doesn't value you because of your gender?

My favorite form of self-harm blossomed as codependency in abusive relationships and developing an addiction to alcohol. The men I chose to marry mirrored the message of women being less than men. I paid dearly for this ideology in the form of domestic violence which eventually led to a diagnosis of complex post-traumatic stress disorder in 2015.

While worldly patriarchal ideology has bled into the culture of The Church of Jesus Christ of Latter-day Saints, I do not get the same message from the doctrine of the Church, the stories of the pioneers, or the presence of Heavenly Mother in the religion.

The Church brought me back to equilibrium with self-love and removed the shame of being female by reframing how I thought about our first mother, Eve. The religion holds deep reverence for Eve's choice as a necessary and hard decision that she had to make to propel the human race forward. Her act was of self-sacrifice and significant foresight.

Priesthood power is our inheritance. The birthright of priesthood power comes from God to the first man, Adam, through Abraham, and to the twelve tribes of Israel. You can see this in Moses 5:4-9, 14-15, and 58-59. Also see Moses 8:16; Abraham 2: 9-11, and Abraham 1:18 and 2:11.

I will be as bold as to say that Eve chose to act under her priesthood power when she made the hard decision for the greater good of all at the expense of receiving hardship and criticism.

Andrew C. Skinner wrote, "The book of Abraham is purposely and completely relevant for our times. It shows us how the Lord has directed several historical threads to converge in these latter days to bring about the restoration of all things. It shows us that the hope in eternity that we today derive from priesthood power, centered in the fulness of the gospel of Jesus Christ, was also the same foundation upon which the ancient patriarchs and matriarchs built their lives."

HEAVENLY MOTHER
Lost in Translation

"We believe the Bible to be the word of God as far
as it is translated correctly; we also believe the Book of
Mormon to be the word of God."
-The 8th Article of Faith,
written in 1842 by the Prophet Joseph Smith

SHEKHINAH

God has many names. It appears our Heavenly Mother is also
called many names in the echoes of the earth's history of religious
belief traced to the very beginning of human existence in ancient
Mesopotamia. The information that has not been destroyed by
worldly patriarchal fear has been buried deep in the ground as relics
of society's past. I began looking into the region where Christianity
originated to see if there existed any evidence of Heavenly Mother
in those cultures. There exists a form of mystical Judaism called
Kabbalism that refers to Heavenly Mother as "Shekhinah."

The book *Wise Women*, edited by Susan Cahill, identifies that
the word "Shekhinah" appears in the Bible referencing a divine
feminine god. It is important for me to quote the first portion of the
section on Judaism from the book:

"The Mother Goddess of the Near East was gradually replaced
by a Father God who became the patriarchal God of the Israelites,

the Christians, and the Muslims, the focus of male-dominant theologies.

"The feminine was not completely suppressed in Judaism, however. It figures in the notion of Shekhinah as the female aspect of God or the name for the manifestation of the sacred presence on earth in the cloud and fire over the Arc of the Covenant, the burning bush, and Mount Sinai. It appears, too in the figure of Hokhmah, the Hebrew embodiment of Wisdom—like the Greek Sophia, feminine in gender—whose female voice is heard in the Wisdom literature of the Bible, excerpted in the following pages.

"Biblical scholar Phyllis Bird, in her essay 'Images of Women in the Old Testament,' points out that 'no single statement can be formulated concerning the image of woman in the Old Testament.' Instead, in texts spanning close to a millennium in their dates of composition (Twelfth to Third Century B.C.), there is a 'plurality of conception.' The creation story of Genesis is only one part of a much longer and complex interaction of God with his creation."

HEROINES & FEMALE RULERS OF ANCIENT TIMES

"Goddess energy is our creative flow: unconditional love, pleasure, passion, and wisdom. When we claim our goddess energy we live in joyful self-acceptance and self-respect, and we listen to our sacred inner voice."
-Heatherash Amara,
Warrior Goddess Training

While searching for resources for this book, I crossed paths with a book called *When Women Ruled the World* by Kara Cooney about the female pharaohs of Ancient Egypt. I am fascinated that there was no alternative title for females in ruling positions. The female was called Pharaoh or King—the same as her male predecessors. The female ruler was commonly holding the seat of power for her son until he came of age.

Egypt was able to become a world power for millennia because the Fertile Crescent allowed an abundance of sustenance for the population in the middle of the desert. The harsh desert terrain kept Egypt from being attacked by outside military forces. An outside force would not have been able to sustain itself for long in that environment. The Egyptians were well taken care of by the growing crops. Coups to overthrow the pharaoh weren't really a thing either.

A system of death ritual was practiced when a pharaoh died. Temporary structures were built resembling temples. Hundreds of people were murdered in these structures to be buried with the pharaoh and accompany him into the afterlife. This mass killing would include advisors, concubines, and even children who were not in line to inherit the throne. Sometimes the wives of the pharaoh would also be killed. All who were ritualistically killed to accompany the pharaoh would be buried in surrounding graves. I believe that this system not only eliminated the competition for the throne but encouraged all members of the pharaoh's family, advisory support, and servants to act in a way that supported the most extended life possible for the current pharaoh.

If the male heir to the throne was not of age to assume the throne, the mother of that male heir would become an interim pharaoh. If this was the case, the mother of the male heir would also decide who would be accompanying the recently deceased pharaoh in his afterlife journey. Having a mother rule until her son came of age was a strategic move in structure because a mother will not act in a way that would harm her son. This was the logic to keeping adult male greed out of the equation. Most adult males who would even desire to usurp would be dead and buried with the previous pharaoh.

When we look at the Ten Commandments, we think "Thou shalt not kill" is a no-brainer. But when Moses brought this commandment forward, it was a radical notion for that time and culture. I am sure that this was especially jarring for the Egyptian royalty, who had been practicing death ritual killings for millennia. Their kingdom and culture were built on a foundation of murder. Moses was raised as an Egyptian, so hearing this commandment out of his mouth is proof of a profound conversion.

Female pharaohs' ruling history was often destroyed and defaced from the walls of structures once her son took his birthright to rule. Even if their rule was recorded in the list of pharaohs in Egyptian historical records, Egyptians were hesitant to allow the stories of successful female leadership to live on.

The mother of the pharaoh was a respected position, and the son would often stay close to his mother's counsel when making decisions as acting pharaoh. This mother-son dynamic at the highest level of kingship was supported by the legends of Egyptian goddesses protecting their sons or working in a way that preserved male pharaohs' right to rule.

In my book, acknowledging that females successfully ruled a large community of people is imperative because women have held so few seats of power or control on earth. Often the female gender is downplayed and dismissed to the point that we have no written accounts of the female experience from their own voices. The stories in the Bible that talk about powerful female characters are still through the filter of male interpretation and language.

It's time to hear, learn from, and include women's spiritual writing in the narrative of collective consciousness. The voices of all the women silenced and burned at the stake are now reverberating through our mouths.

When I first knew for myself that a divine feminine energy or ruler existed, I was sitting in an intuition class about a year before

I was baptized. The intuition class was led by a beautifully gifted psychic empath and transformational coach. I saw a flash of Heavenly Mother's face. I was taken back by Her and started asking questions. A few days after I saw Heavenly Mother's face, I was commissioned to photograph maternity images for a woman I did not know.

I arrived at the pregnant woman's location, ready for the photoshoot. I began talking to her and her sister, who were members of the Church of Jesus Christ of Latter-day Saints. I was raised predominantly born-again Christian, and talking about a female version of God was always cast as "blasphemy." I hesitantly approached the subject of my vision during the intuition workshop with these women. I already felt like I was walking a fine line of cognitive dissonance with my attendance because I was talking about a seminar led by a psychic. Any talk of paganism or psychic involvement with Christians usually does not end well.

They were both very loving and accepting of me talking about my experience seeing Heavenly Mother and told me that the LDS religion recognized Her existence. Seeds were planted in me that day.

I have had the spiritual gift of vision my whole life. After diving into family history, I have learned that these gifts run in my male and female family lines. I have been a "seer" of visions of the future, ideas in dreams, visions of spirits of the dead, beings of light, and demonic entities holding dominion over spaces and demons that inhabit the bodies of individuals they have made contracts with.

As I have "cleaned up" my energy by overcoming an addiction to alcohol, healing trauma, and progressing spiritually, my gifts have become more robust. I am more attuned to energy and the voice of a Heavenly Mother. I have had two visions of our divine mother since receiving my endowments and claiming my priesthood power. She is regal, tall, bold, and looks like me in those visions. Many women I have spoken to who have seen Her have said, "That's so funny because when I see Her, She looks like me!"

Heavenly Mother choosing to appear to women as a mirror of themselves is no coincidence.

HONOR THY MOTHER

We know Heavenly Mother exists; we want a relationship with her. But we don't know enough about how to find Her to connect with Her. If you're going to connect with Mother, look no farther than the experiences you have with your own body.

Heavenly Mother is in the physical manifestation of creation. She is in the way we experience the presence of God with our bodies. We honor Her by taking care of our bodies. We can keep Her close to us with body movement, using our bodies for sound (singing, speaking), and somatic nervous system regulation by interacting with the rhythms and energy of the earth itself.

We honor Her with exercise to combat illnesses and ailments of all kinds. We heal our relationship with Her when we heal our generational traumas or life traumas. We honor Her by taking care of the physical world for future generations. We honor Heavenly Mother when we care about good stewardship of blessings, maintenance of temples, and the earth.

Our somatic nervous system is a system that transmits information back and forth between the central nervous system (CNS) and the rest of the body. The somatic nervous system contains two major types of neurons. Different neurons are responsible for carrying information from the body to the central nervous system. Motor neurons carry information from the brain and spinal cord to muscle fibers.

Neurons that make up the somatic nervous system project outwards from the CNS connect directly to the body's muscles and carry signals from muscles and sensory organs back to the CNS.

The neuron's body in the CNS and the axon (a portion of the neuron that carries nerve impulses away from the cell body) then projects and terminates in the skin, sensory organs, or muscles.

MY NATURAL PROGRESSION OF THOUGHTS:

Reflexes = neural pathway = reflex arc
The word was God,
God was the word,
God's intent and words organized matter into the world we live on,
Word + voice resonance = vibrations
Acoustic sound resonance studies by Stanford on the human heart cells,
The words we speak with our voice resonance can cause life or death to the heart cells of others because of our intentions,
Sound bowl acoustic vibrations and resonance (hertz),
Crystal and natural stone formations holding different vibrations,
Body responding to vibrational energy,
Healing tissue and disease with vibrational resonance,
Emotional roots to body disease,
"Words like violence."

HOW WORLDLY PATRIARCHY HAD PERVERTED
HEAVENLY MOTHER'S CONTRIBUTION

- By disrespecting women's contributions to the world.
- Turning ancient practices of connecting to earth into "occult" and killing women, such as divination tools, dancing, and practicing healing.
  - Divination tools such as: writing, oracle/tarot cards, various forms of seership, music

107

- Not giving women credit for their work in literature.
- Female Viking warrior graves were construed as males by archaeologists.
- Scientific studies with research bias on how certain disorders impact males and not females OR only basing female diagnoses on male displays of these disorders.
- Mental asylums admitting women for not being obedient to men and a myriad of other heinous reasons.
- Prostitution in the early West expected to give massive amounts of money to the community, but they were not able to be buried in the same cemeteries as the townspeople.
- Female pharaohs' written histories were destroyed once their sons came of age to claim the throne.

SACRED GEOMETRY
& THE PHYSICAL WORLD

The most sacred geometry is the female body. Some of my sacred rages will now be transmuted into words to demand more.

Before we get into the body of the information I was divinely guided to on sacred geometry, I want to address the contribution of male members of the Church to the toxic church culture dynamic. I am also going to drag the issue of domestic violence into the light.

I am a survivor of domestic violence and hear about these issues happening in the homes of current members. Some men are still hiding in the darkness. Pornography and physical abuse in a relationship ignite a sacred rage in me.

I want to be very clear and draw some lines in the sand with you who believe that an addiction to pornography or abusive behavioral pattern is just a part of your identity. This is to those of you who think and say that these behaviors are tolerable and allow them into your homes, minds, limiting beliefs, and your children's environment.

It is futile to believe that you can wear a church face and have a different identity in your home. Several women I have spoken to that have left the Church did so because of the double lives of male priesthood holders who exercised unrighteous dominion over their families.

How you treat women says more about you than the boxes checked on your religious attendance and what you say you believe. How you handle the sacred vessel which manifests new souls to this plane of existence says more about how you honor your God(s) than anything else you could do with your life.

Can you imagine that God loved man SO much that he fashioned a companion specifically for you, and you spit in His face by treating your woman poorly?

Can you imagine how insulted your God is when you betray her? When you force her to choose between you and her? When you abandon her in moments of need for your own selfish impulse?

Men have no idea what the experience of being at the physical mercy of a man is like for women. Men have no idea what degrees of suffering it takes to birth, to look at your own blood every month. You have no clue what it is like to watch your hands fill with your own life force because a man couldn't control his temper and then lashed out to destroy a part of your flesh. Such acts instinctually tie doubt in the woman's mind toward God the Father.

For women, their blood becomes a unit of measurement of tolerance. She learns her body with the sacrifices, waxing and waning each moon cycle. She is the ship riding on blood tides to deliver the children of men safely to shore.

Men, if you are serious about your church disciplines, you must claim ownership and mastery of delayed gratification. You must be better about holding a safe space for us to produce abundance, share our stories, and develop better policies and checks and balances for the seats of power over entire populations in this Church.

Women in sacred covenants with men of the Church are not being respected, and we are evolving past you as a result. The energetic dynamic is too unbalanced, causing women to rise into their masculine energy that drives female contribution to the toxic aspects of church culture.

To my sisters struggling in relationships that are causing you to spiritually hemorrhage your energetic lifeforce—stop giving a man the power of God over you. Stop right now. Make that decision to collect back the parts of you that are indissoluble. Do it unapologetically. In your stance to claim your life as your own and say, "ENOUGH." Exercise your priesthood power. If the power dynamic is askew in your relationship with your man, he is not your divinely appointed equal partner.

Period.

You are entitled to this sacred rage because the higher part of you tells you that you deserve better than your current circumstances. Any emotion can be a catalyst for positive change. If we are serious about spiritual growth in The Church of Jesus Christ of Latter-day Saints, we have to be serious about accountability. You are entitled to hold your partner accountable. You are entitled to true, safe intimacy. We have to feel safe being vulnerable in our marriage. If he is not safe for you to unfurl to, he must be held accountable.

The belief of the martyred suffering of the wife for a man's sins is a mechanism of worldly Western ideology that has integrated into the Church and is still keeping all of us (men and women) small. This is another device of shame from the adversary.

The belief you must suffer for the glory or protection of your man is seared into the false narrative of your conditioning and it can neurologically be rewired to claim the fierce light warrior within you. If you are demographically a white, middle-aged female, this is primarily a case of self-harm as found from studies in the book *When She Was Bad* by Patricia Pearson. Worldly patriarchy has hardwired us to modes of self-harm as labels of loyalty to men who have no interest in protecting us.

I had the following download into my mind about leaning into God when we feel lost as women. When we feel lost, we are supposed to turn to God over men as a replacement for a husband because human men are limited and designated to a more physical or tactile purpose than women. They are different creatures from us with other purposes energetically. They cannot hold the overflow when we are in states of emotional destruction or our chaos phases that mimic cycles of natural chaos you see in the physical world. Women energetically and physically emulate the same cycles of creation and destruction synced monthly with the moon cycles. We hold a gravitational pull because of the way our bodies and emotions are designed that only other women and our Heavenly Parents can grasp. The connective community of women we are a part of is so imperative to us.

The human male can hold safe physical and emotional space with an enlightened mind. This will allow the female to exercise her unapologetic power of womb creation energy in all aspects of the couple's life. Sometimes this sacred power of womb creation requires whole armies of men to adequately protect her so that she can open her creative capacity to its fullest potential.

The spiritual army of human males assigned to hold space for us women to claim our priesthood power consists of the prophet, the apostles, and the quorums of seventy that sit at the head of leadership of the Church. They are literally creating spaces of intimacy and safety to connect with our Heavenly Parents and receive personal revelation.

The direct instruction of the current prophet, Russell M. Nelson, called me into the Church. In a general conference talk, he said that we are all responsible for gathering the lost tribes of Israel and it shot me like an arrow into my heart. I knew he was speaking to me through the television that day. I knew I was a part of something greater than myself at that moment. I decided to pursue becoming a member of the Church because of how the Holy Spirit moved through me in President Russell M. Nelson's call to action. I knew that if I didn't become a member and rise to my full stature, there would be people who would not actualize their potential. I knew that if I did not speak, certain people would not hear.

I understood at that moment that God had kept me alive through domestic violence, insurmountable odds, and my own reckless life decisions to create a massive tsunami of change for the better.

The prophet also tasked women to truly understand what it means for us to hold priesthood power. I took that so seriously that I decided to accept God's calling for me to write this book about what female priesthood power in The Church of Jesus Christ of Latter-day Saints truly means.

God needs to be involved in marriage to hold the expansion of capacity for female creation of abundance. He is the ultimate lover and pursuer. He must maintain us the same way He has our Heavenly Mother at times.

As the pinnacle of divine husbandry, God represents the essence we need to lean into when human men fail us. We must rely on God when men fail us because God has promised His duty to us as sacred daughters, made in the image of His ultimate beloved— Heavenly Mother. We are the bride of the living God, the holy bodies of the living Church.

I want to express my love for men at this point. Enlightened men are NOT less than us, and women who wish to have equal respect only wish to rule in alignment with men. We do not want control over men. We want equal partnership and safety. I believe that we are more sacred vessels than men simply because of our unique capabilities to birth unique 3D creations. No, I am not only talking about the capability to birth physical babies. We gestate and deliver in various capacities aside from giving birth to children.

Whenever we marry the subconscious raw power of the human mind with the superconscious mind, which can also be called the "will of God," we are able to magnetize Source energy to us.

Heavenly Mother steps in at this point in the form of physics to marry God power with earth matter and human beings can manifest miracles, work, art, etc. The divine marriage of masculine and feminine energy within our earthly being is then harnessed and we become co-creators with our Heavenly Parents.

"Like God we can become." We are made in God's image. The capacity that we possess to create from atoms and materials already available in the universe keeps us in line with our Heavenly Parents. When we are disciplined with adherence to our covenants, we possess more full manifestation and healing capabilities. The Church of Jesus Christ of Latter-day Saints teaches a lot about "HOW" with rules and practical applications. But there is not enough about the "WHY" and intuition of "HOW" adherence blesses us. Intuition and revelation development is mainly left to the individual members to stumble through with hopes to catch on.

Education about Heavenly Mother, the use of the body to promote wellness, and eradicating stigmatization around human females actualizing their power would propel the trajectory of the Church to reach its full stature on this earth.

The systems and space already in place like cocoons to hold the soul metamorphosis of its members is magnificent. All I see is this Church's potential to make Joseph Smith's prophecies a reality.

The Church of Jesus Christ of Latter-day Saints can still evolve. Rising in vibration to enact the necessary changes for all members of the Church is imperative if we truly desire to experience the divine marriage of current church principles with transformation on a global scale.

Spiritual law can trump karmic laws with the application of faith through the raw force of the human subconscious mind. As Florence Scovel Shinn asserted, "Life is not a battle, it is a game. Life is a game that becomes more clear on how to play with the rules of spiritual law."

Faith is a form of surrender or "letting go" that is required to clear the emotional clutter of doubt, shame, and negativity so that we have room to receive divine intervention on our behalf. Sacred geometry allows us to glimpse into the heavenly energetic light bodies that harbor actual change.

The High Priestess

SACRED GEOMETRY

Image of the vesica piscis, designed by Mike Bryant:

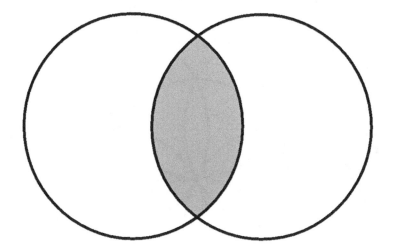

I had a symbol of two circles intersecting tattooed on my neck with a rune symbolizing fertility during a time in my life when I was struggling with fertility issues and miscarriage. I am primarily Celtic in my genetic makeup and I had the tattoo ink a blue color that mimicked the ancient Pict women of the Celtic region. At the time that I had it tattooed on me, I did not realize what this symbol was.

I had this symbol flash into my mind one day when I was sitting down to research information for this book. I looked it up and started laughing out loud. The two circles overlapping are called the vesica piscis. One circle represents spirit, heaven, and males. The other circle represents matter, earth, and females. The spiritual meaning

117

of the vesica piscis is the union of opposites. The symbol is the Mother of Geometry or the Symbol of the Divine Feminine.

The mathematical "phi" derives from this. "The Golden Ratio," a system of proportion often used in nature to guide the growth of plants and animals, also derives from the Mother of Geometry.

Image of the Seed of Life, designed by Mike Bryant:

Three pairs of these sets combined within one larger circle is called the Seed of Life—an ancient geometric rosette with 18 lens-shaped petals: 6 smaller ones inside and 12 larger ones outside. My personal observation is that the seed of life looks like a human egg in the first stages of fertilization.

Image of the Flower of Life, designed by Mike Bryant:

The Seed of Life multiplied creates the Flower of Life. The Flower of Life is a net of interlocking circles and rosettes. It is constructed of 19 circles. Euclid, the "father of geometry," would use the Flower of Life to create all geometric figures by hand.

The Seed of Life is related to the numbers 6 and 7, which appear to have significant meanings in Christian religions and scriptures. I made the connection of 6 main energy centers or chakras in the body with the 7th chakra being the crown chakra. Also, God made the earth in six days, and on the seventh day, He rested.

You can also see geometric progression in metaphysics with the stellated octahedron. The Merkaba is the shape created by crossing two tetrahedrons. The Seed of Life and the Merkaba come from six-sided geometry.

Image of Merkaba, designed by Mike Bryant:

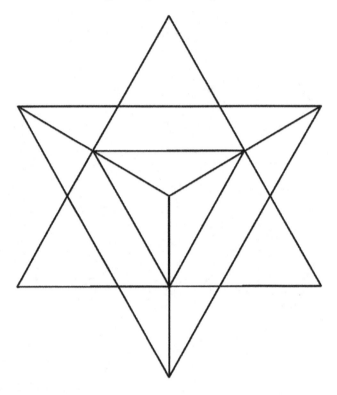

In Hebrew, Merkaba (also spelled Merkabah or Merkava) means "chariot." The word originally referred to the moving throne of God in the Bible. For example, the vision of Ezekiel and the spiritual practices based on that vision.

When operating in the metaphysical world, the Merkaba is a restructuring of the energy body represented by a series of stellated, spinning octahedrons. The belief is that the Merkaba is aligned with the main chakras along the spine. It is below the feet chakras and ends just above the crown chakra.

Heavenly Mother is the mother of geometry—the mother of the physical world we now inhabit. The Seed of Life and Merkaba have become personal and collective evolution symbols. The mother of geometry is proof of our Heavenly Mother and Her dominion. It is not a coincidence that the point where the two circles intersect is the same shape as female human anatomy. In those six days of creation, I wonder how much physical labor Heavenly Mother must have endured giving birth to this world we live on.

More on Merkaba:

The Merkaba is the vehicle of light composed of male and female united energies that, when combined, allow an individual to ascend to higher states of consciousness. This unity of balanced, divine powers within the body enables us to experience a personal revelation. The Flower of Life or "mother of geometry" is a blueprint of all living things that remind us we are all connected by origin from the same Divine Mother.

The High Priestess

TIL DEATH DO US PART

The practice of eternal marriage in the Church of Jesus Christ of Latter-day Saints is distinctive from other branches of Christianity. A type of priesthood power is the sealing or joining of individual priesthood power with another priesthood holder in the temple's crowning ordinance of sealing. The sealing ordinance allows us to be with our spouse and children for all time and eternity.

Together with a spouse, we can bring children into the world that are also covered by this eternal covenant we make with each other. The sealing allows us to be together as a family in the afterlife.

Many belief systems outside of the Church of Jesus Christ of Latter-day Saints address "soul ties" in the form of sexual intimacy or verbal vows tying souls together. These beliefs are similar to views in the Church that seek to add additional safeguards toward guarding sexual intimacy. These safeguards look like spiritual laws of chastity that members are encouraged to follow. Keeping family units together is of utmost importance.

I had been married three times before my marriage to my current husband. All of those marriages were civil marriages. In my vows, I used the words "until death do us part" in each of those marriages. Civil marriage and my divorces were governed by the jurisdiction of the state I was married in.

President Hinckley gave a talk during his life about the contrast between civil marriage and celestial marriage. In that talk, President Hinckley recanted an instance where he spoke with a newly married couple at the opening of a temple. He illustrated that when the couple gave their vows of "'til death do us part," they also sealed the time of their separation from one another. The state is not ordained by God to seal couples together past the bonds of death.

In that way, the Atonement of Jesus Christ allows us to overcome the severance of the soul tie beyond death. The Atonement, combined with the authority of the temple sealing, will enable us to be tied to our spouse through the veil when one passes away before the other.

There is a logical headspace where I can explain all of this to you as I understand it. But the cellular level of understanding of this logic came to me on February 3, 2022. This date brought an experience like a gut punch that tempered a cavern of understanding of the difference.

In February 2022, I received word that my ex-husband had passed away a few days prior. My relationship with him was turbulent and I experienced domestic violence at his hands. Most people experience the loss of a loved one, but losing enemies is a unique experience. To the date of writing this book, my ex-husband is the second person in five years who had wished death on me and is no longer living. I still experienced grief, which was an unexpected emotional space. I also felt relieved that he was gone.

Changes began taking place in my body that started a series of pressure releases. The release of tension from my muscles started from my face and slowly worked down my entire body over the next couple of days. I had experienced constant tightness in my neck and my shoulders to the degree that chiropractors couldn't relieve it for more than a couple of days. But now I felt lighter in my body.

I had experienced physical and mental abuse in that marriage. I have been carrying around pain from the harm he had imposed upon me for almost five years. Fear began leaving my body in a way that made me feel like gravity had shifted. I felt weightless as I adjusted to his absence.

I was sitting in my car, processing the news of his passing, when I heard my own voice say, "'Til death do us part."

My testimony of celestial marriage started at this juncture. I said, "Oh, THAT is what that means." What I had been experiencing in my body over a couple of days was the release of the verbal vow I had made to him. The oral contract and soul tie no longer bound me to him once he passed away. I now had a visceral comprehension of the difference between civil marriage and celestial marriage.

The newfound lightness was present in my body and my countenance and attitude. God revealed in prayer that the innocence I had walled up to protect myself in that relationship was now safe to come out. Now I am striving and asking God for answers on innocence's impact on the physical body and healing cells. Children possess higher purity, stem cells, and faith levels than adults. I believe that using innocence in the repentance, humility, and conversion processes is what Jesus meant when He said, "Be ye as the little children."

Let us go down the path of this bizarre coming of consciousness. About a month after my ex-husband's passing, I participated in a healing practice with my coach, Keira Poulsen. We were asking for the healing of bitterness, rage, and resentment. I had gone through some tough days the week before this healing.

An aspect of having trauma in my past is that my mind can only play blips of specific trauma memories. I had memories of the sound of abuse coming up. The sounds were of my own screams and pleading in situations where I was being abused. I heard the cracks of my own bones hitting tile or walls and I heard tissue throbbing in my ears. It was similar to when I have a song playing on repeat on my stereo. Only the stereo was a recall of war cries—animalistic sounds of survival. I heard my cries over and over again.

My throat tightened like it was caught in a noose during the healing. I didn't understand it. I felt like I was breathing fire like a dragon. I felt resistance.

Take a dance class if you ever want to work on trust-building exercises with your spouse or significant other. The resistance was similar to when I took dance lessons with my husband. My husband and I were beginning to learn the tango in this scenario. The male is supposed to lead the female in the dance steps. The simple manipulation of my body with his body was so difficult for me as a woman who has been through domestic violence. I have similar safety issues with obedience to being led by outside sources.

When I left the healing exercise with Keira that night, I was frustrated that I was not relieved. I was hard on myself, thinking I may have done things wrong in my part of the exercise. The point of healing isn't always to have instant relief, though. Think about the process of healing a deep burn or road rash. A wire brush is taken for road rash to get all of the debris out of the skin to stave off infection. During the healing process of burns, the wounds have to be scrubbed to keep them clean. This is not an easy process for the injured person. But the debris has to come out to promote a healthy, energetic body. Energetic healing is similar to the grueling process our bodies have to go through. It's not always easy or instant or fun.

I had a vision during the healing exercise that I will share with you as I received and wrote it down.

VISUAL DURING HEALING EXERCISE:

An empty airport.

A vastness of negative space.

An amber glow of light penetrates the gray inside the building.

It's the light of a sunrise.

A new day has been given to me.

I am content.

I am content to be who I am.

I am content with myself.

I am content with my thoughts.

Weary no more.

Fueled by travel and why I am moving along.

The next steps are always under me.

I am assured.

I am before me.

The steps.

Under me.

Divinely placed like the purpose-driven life

I chose to run toward it.

Sure footing.

I walk toward the gate of my flight.

There He is.

He is happy to receive me.

He has been saving me a seat next to Him.

He reaches for me and laces my fingers with His.

The ultimate lover of me.

Is my God.

Safety,

Legacy,

Provision,

Precision.

God as my travel companion.
Hand in Hand.
Intimacy in a movement,
That is quicker than a walk with Him.
He whispers in my ear,
"You are mine."

The day following this exercise.

I WEEP
&
Weep.

MY TESTIMONY ON APRIL 10, 2022 AND IN CLOSE OF THIS BOOK

I have been burning with several testimonies this week and had to write them down.

I will share one of the testimonies strengthened this week.

My testimony is that I know that Joseph Smith was a prophet who was given the vision of the highest potential of this Church.

I need to give some context about the refining conversion in my life. Even granting this testimony is a miracle happening in front of your eyes. But you would dismiss this miracle as a common Fast Sunday confession if I don't share my heart with you. Let this be a lesson to you that miracles happen every day in front of you but are disguised as the "norm." All you have to do is attune your awareness to see the miracles.

I was raised by a mother who left the Church. Subsequently, she continued in contention with her father about this decision. The hardships in their relationship were initiated by him.

My grandfather was in a car accident on a ski trip when he was 33 years old and became a quadriplegic. After my studies on traumatic brain injury, I believe that much of his behavior toward my mother resulted from this life-altering occurrence.

The contention and constant arguing between my mother and grandfather was an energetic sound bath that my young body and mind marinated in at any family function. They both brought their trauma and pride to the dinner table. My cells and the water within my body trapped these intentions. However, I also want to highlight the gifts they gave me through this process as all aspects of our lives provide strength. Both my mother and my grandfather taught me how to stand up for what I believe is right. They also taught me how to sit in the uncomfortable aspects of life and keep showing up. Remember—showing up is 90% of the battle.

I recently learned that the human voice has more resonance on bodily tissue than a sound bowl. Stanford University did a study on heart cells when exposed to acoustic sound and found that sound can change the geometric patterns of the heart cells. What does that say about the power of our words and choosing to speak life toward one another? A little food for thought.

I also grew up in a small town that was predominantly LDS. I experienced the sharpening aspects of being a social pariah throughout my adolescence because I was a born-again Christian, not a member of the Church. The actions of the members and their children toward me reinforced what my mother was saying. An African proverb says, "The child who is not embraced by the village will burn it down to feel its warmth."

Added to this hatred of the culture that members have adopted over time was a disdain for everything I was taught about Joseph Smith. I carried a hatred for Joseph Smith in my heart throughout my life and judged Mormons along the way. Believe me, the culture of the members to this day still tests Jesus within me. We're still a long way off from the heart space of energetic harmony that would raise this Church to new heights.

These limiting beliefs about Joseph Smith and judging people in the Church helped me feel in alignment with my mother. It also made me no better than that which I hated. As a true Benjamite, I fed and justified my wickedness into enormous manifestations of sin in my life before God had enough and put my face to the ground. As you can tell, I share a tribe with Ehud and the Apostle Paul.

Here enters the Holy Spirit's influence. I always see, hear, and feel the Holy Spirit like water. It's usually raining down in rooms. On occasion, the Holy Spirit will pour. It can clear like a fast river. With me, it persistently wore away at my hardened resolve as water wears away rock over the years.

I've always had access to my spiritual gifts. It was more a matter of what I was using them for. I had always felt the Holy Spirit even when making my bed in hell.

Priesthood power was given to us to perform healing and miracles in this realm of existence when we feel prompted to act under love or the highest good. If only worthy LDS people could experience the Holy Spirit, I would not be here. The gift of the Holy Spirit conferred during my confirmation was something besides the initial granting of access. I believe my confirmation has to do with physics. I believe the confirmation ordinance is how we can eventually harness the priesthood power very quickly.

The Holy Spirit is a conduit of closing space and time for understanding. For example, I can instantly KNOW something due to the Holy Spirit that logically should have taken years of earthly experience to learn.

I could tell you many scientific facts about how it is now believed that water carries information and intentions inside of it, but I will save that for another time. But there was definitely a noticeable shift in my confirmation dealing with the Holy Spirit. Maybe it's the difference between a drizzle to a downpour?

I will tell you that the ordinances of this Church are strong enough to hold safe, sacred space for the profound energetic transfigurations or conversions needed to grow you through your carnal man into your highest self or your soul's purpose in this life. These ordinances also begin a process of healing on cellular levels and align us with body healing.

Going back to Joseph Smith—I hated him due to the environmental aspect and experiences of my upbringing. I conceded that he was most likely a prophet if God demanded me to become a member of this Church.

So, I was baptized. I began gaining my testimony that he was a prophet over COVID in profound ways that God knows only I'd understand. Recently, my testimony that Joseph Smith is a prophet was solidified by no less than an ex-member of this Church. There's some irony for you.

I testify that Joseph Smith was aligned with Jesus Christ as he sought to not just restore the Church on earth. But he also shared company with our Savior in the energetic space of elevating women. One step further, Joseph Smith endeavored to promote women in a way that defied worldly patriarchy. We are still not to our prophet's highest ideal for this Church and we are running out of time to gather the rest of scattered Israel.

I also testify that even our darkest hardships become tools for our purpose. I am grateful to my mother for her convictions because it allowed me to think critically and find answers. My mother has a brilliant mind and taught me to seek all answers for myself. I am thankful to have been an outcast growing up because it will enable me to hold firm against the faith crises I cycle into when I experience the injurious behaviors of toxic church culture toward my family and myself.

I am grateful to be in the company of Jesus and empathize with his walk of being an outsider. I am grateful for my experience before my conversion, which allows me to understand the pain people experience when they act from a place of trauma. We must understand the darkness in us to have the bravery to bring the light of Christ into the lives of others. I am grateful for my life because it has led me here to a place of claiming my birthright. I am grateful to be alive and a member of this Church. I am thankful to be what I am.

I testify to you that desecration, denigration, and deviation of Joseph Smith's original reception methods of divine understanding are becoming sacrilegious. He pushes us from across the veil to come back to his vision and remember the origins of the covenant path.

I testify that if you continue to walk forward with questions and faith, regardless of whether you're worthy, God will not fail you to answer. If you step forward with your sincere desire for a testimony, you will gain one.

The world showed me what I was willing to die for. I testify that the Church has raised my standards, shown me what I am living for, and helped me to be restored to myself.

I ask that God will wrap this book in light and that Jesus will make Himself known in a tangible way to all who read it. I pray that Heavenly Mother will manifest this book into the hands of the women and men who need it, into the hands of the leaders who can create positive change, and that the Holy Spirit will provide the necessary understanding to the souls of all those who seek to understand. I ask that the energy of the words in this book will manifest this book into the hands of anyone who needs it, even if they have no money to buy it. I ask through the light of Christ that the energy of this book will make it hard to find for those who seek to tear the truth from the light. I ask for the Archangel Michael to protect this book and carry its intentions safely where it needs to go.

Lord, I ask that You grace me with continuous power. I ask that the light of Christ will pour through the top of my head through my mind and all of my body to rearrange my cells for long life. I am asking for full-body health and healing so that my body may carry the seeds of truth to more souls.

I ask that all of my ancestors, angels, and the ascended masters who have been assigned to me to direct me toward my highest good will continue to hold space and time for me to complete my soul's purpose on this earth. The work of the soul is sacred.

I testify, petition, and close my book in and through the light of our beautiful Savior, Jesus Christ.

AMEN.

ARE YOU STRUGGLING WITH YOUR TESTIMONY? ASK YOURSELF THESE QUESTIONS AND WRITE THE ANSWERS IN YOUR JOURNAL.

1. Do you want a testimony? If the answer is "no" then what resistance do you notice coming up to the surface? Does it have an underlying memory tied to it?
2. What areas of your beliefs and current testimony are you struggling with?
3. Write down the questions you have for our Heavenly Parents about these areas of uncertainty.

EXERCISE

Carve out 15 minutes. Go to a quiet place and open your hands in a show of openness to receive. Open your heart with prayer and ask those questions you wrote down. Say, "Through the Light of Christ, reveal the answers to me," before you close this prayer. Now admit to yourself that it is okay not to have all of the answers right now.

A TIP FOR YOU ON RECEIVING ANSWERS

Release the expectations of what those answers must look like. They may come in the form of a homeless man or a word jumping out at you on the page of a newspaper you walk by. The answer may be through the appearance of an animal or in a whisper in the wind that only you can hear.

Sometimes we get distracted by the need for external validation. When you feel the truth of the answer to your question, accept it for what it is, NOT what you want it to be. If you find it hard to get and wonder, "Is this from God or is this my own mind trying to make this fit into my own personal narrative," close your eyes and ask inwardly by tapping lightly on your chest with your fingers and asking if the answer was from God. Inherently, you already know.

All of the answers to our questions are already within our eternal souls.

LDS CONCEPTS AS DEFINED BY MID-LIFE CONVERT, LINDSEY A. BRYANT:

Atonement: The eradication of the need for maintaining blood sacrifices made possible by the sacrifice of Jesus Christ which covered our sins from the point of Jesus' death through the reverberation of the remainder of time. The Atonement was paid by the high value of the blood of Jesus relinquishing laws of karma to laws of grace. The freedom of the blood of Jesus paid human ransom to the laws of karma. Karma dictates, "An eye for an eye" or "What goes around comes around." The payment of Jesus' blood freed humans so we can overcome the body's physical death and the soul death's from sinful behavior.

Covenant Keeping: Alignment reward system of regulated dopamine releases to carve new neurological pathways into the brain which builds confidence and promotes greater longevity of cells toward a longer life on earth in order to fulfill one's highest purpose.

Forgiveness: The transmutation of negative energy into positive motivation toward an external, healthy coping mechanism so that pain no longer lives in your body to impact your health negatively.

Jesus: A metaphysician and Son of God who emphasized the use of verbal intent to harness the power of God toward healing the physical body and performing miracles. Characterized as "the Lamb of God" because His sacrifice of blood was the most valuable payment toward the sins of man. Jesus' blood was so valuable because of how energetically clean He was. His ability to master the human condition accounted for His metaphysical abilities.

Love and Forgiveness: Selfless states of energetic clearing of tension from the mind and body which allows freedom from the impulsive reaction of external stimulus. Transitions an individual from a masculine energetic reactive state of mind to an internal feminine energetic state of intuitive knowing and observing.

Priesthood Power of Women: Exercising access to the physics of God's power as a vehicle to deliver healing to others, banish demons or the devil from spaces, self-healing, and, ultimately, bring miracles of abundant love to earth. Doing so free from fear of punishment, retribution, or bodily harm.

Sin: Another binding element toward the human condition that distinguishes how humans are separate from God. God is not bound by the carnal desires or needs that lead humans toward sinful activity and distraction from pure love and purpose. Sin is also a method of causing the nervous system to be unregulated and a breach of spiritual contractual agreement that causes an individual to become out of alignment energetically. This can cause physical tension and potential illness. It is selfishness, NOT to be confused with self-care methods.

Self-Care Methods: Self-care methods regulate the nervous system, align chakras, and allow reception in a divine feminine energetic state of reception to receive personal revelation. See studies on breakthroughs or solutions being found in states of play or taking a break in silence, meditation, and singing.

Time: An element of temporary binding of the human condition. The purpose of time is to learn how to make use of time correctly toward one's life purpose. Time is also a degree of separation from God because God is not bound by time. He is external from it.

The High Priestess

REFERENCES

Bednar, David A. "Things as They Really Are." The Church of Jesus Christ of Latter-day Saints. Accessed May 9, 2022. https://www.churchofjesuschrist.org/study/ensign/2010/06/things-as-they-really-are?lang=eng.

Cacioppo, S., Frum, C., Asp, E., Weiss, R. M., Lewis, J. W., & Cacioppo, J. T. "A quantitative meta-analysis of functional imaging studies of social rejection." 2013.

Chopra, Deepak, and Menas C Kafatos. *You Are the Universe: Discovering Your Cosmic Self and Why It Matters*. Harmony, 2017.

Estés, Clarissa Pinkola. *Women Who Run with the Wolves: Myths and Stories of the Wild Woman Archetype*. New York: Ballantine Books, 1992.

Huson, Barbara (previously Barbara Stanny). *Sacred Success: A Course in Financial Miracles*. BenBella Books, 2014.

Nelson, Russell M. "A Plea to My Sisters." The Church of Jesus Christ of Latter-day Saints. Accessed May 9, 2022. https://www.churchofjesuschrist.org/study/general-conference/2015/10/a-plea-to-my-sisters?lang=eng.

Pearson, Patricia. *When She Was Bad: Violent Women & the Myth of Innocence*. New York, NY: Viking, 1997.

"Power - Definition, Meaning & Synonyms." Vocabulary.com. Accessed May 9, 2022. https://www.vocabulary.com/dictionary/power.

Radke, S., Jankowiak, K., Tops, S., Abel, T., Habel, U., & Derntl, B. (2021). "Neurobiobehavioral responses to virtual social rejection in females—exploring the influence of oxytocin." *Social Cognitive and Affective Neuroscience*, Volume 16 (December 2020): 326–333. https://doi.org/10.1093/scan/nsaa168

Seagraves, Anne. *Soiled Doves: Prostitution in the Early West*. Hayden, ID: Wesanne Publications, 1994.

Slavich, G. M., O'Donovan, A., Epel, E. S., & Kemeny, M. E. (2010). "Black sheep get the blues: a psychobiological model of social rejection and depression." *Neuroscience and Biobehavioral Reviews*, Volume 35 (September 2010): 39–45. https://doi.org/10.1016/j.neubiorev.2010.01.003

Skinner, Andrew C. "The Book of Abraham: A Most Remarkable Book." The Ensign, Volume 27, No. 3 (March 1997): pp.16-23.

Smith, Mataeo. "What Is the Law of Vibration?" The US Sun. The US Sun, October 20, 2021. https://www.the-sun.com/lifestyle/3897774/what-is-the-law-of-vibration/.

Tamur, Erhan. "She Who Wrote: Enheduanna and Women of Mesopotamia, Ca. 3400–2000 BC (October 15, 2022 through February 19, 2023)." The Morgan Library & Museum, October 11, 2021. https://www.themorgan.org/blog/she-who-wrote-enheduanna-and-women-mesopotamia.

Toone, Trent. "10 Remarkable Women in LDS Church History." Deseret News. Deseret News, May 7, 2014. https://www.deseret.com/2014/5/7/20540994/10-remarkable-women-in-lds-church-history.

Turley, Richard E., and Brittany A. Chapman. *Women of Faith in the Latter Days, Vol. 3: 1846-1870*. Deseret Book, 2014.

Thank you for reading my book! I would be SO grateful if you would head over to Amazon, or wherever you found this and leave a review!
-Lindsey Bryant

Made in the USA
Las Vegas, NV
06 June 2022